Space and Astronomy

49 Science Fair Projects

Other Books in the
Science Fair Projects Series

BOTANY
49 Science Fair Projects (No. 3277)
This first volume in the series concentrates on plant germination, photosynthesis, hydroponics, plant tropism, plant cells, seedless plants, and plant dispersal.

EARTH SCIENCE
49 Science Fair Projects (No. 3287)
This second volume in the series concentrates on Earth's meteorology and oceanography, as well as the Earth's crust, weather, solar energy, acid rain, fossils, and rocks and minerals.

ENVIRONMENTAL SCIENCE
49 Science Fair Projects (No. 3369)
This third volume in the series deals with Earth's surroundings and how pollution, waste disposal, irrigation, erosion, and heat and light affect the ecology.

COMPUTERS
49 Science Fair Projects (No. 3524)
This fourth volume in the series integrates computers with science, applying scientific principles to games of chance, aircraft design, calculating energy costs, forecasting weather, calculating odds, and making mathematical conversions.

BOTANY
49 MORE Science Fair Projects (No. 3416)
This fifth volume in the series expounds the exciting experiments in the very first book in the series. It contains experiments in plant germination, photosynthesis, hydroponics, plant tropism, plant cells, seedless plants, and plant dispersal.

Science Fair
Projects

S e r i e s

Space and Astronomy

49 Science Fair Projects

Robert L. Bonnet
G. Daniel Keen

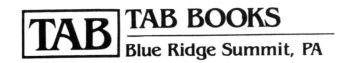

TAB BOOKS
Blue Ridge Summit, PA

FIRST EDITION
FIRST PRINTING

© 1992 by **TAB Books**.
TAB Books is a division of McGraw-Hill, Inc.

Library of Congress Cataloging-in-Publication Data

Bonnet, Robert L.
    Aeronautics and space : 49 science fair projects / by Robert L. Bonnet and G. Daniel Keen.
        p.   cm.
    Includes index.
    Summary: Suggests a variety of astronomy projects suitable for science fairs, involving the stars, moon, planets, and Milky Way.
    ISBN 0-8306-3939-X   ISBN 0-8306-3938-1 (pbk.)
    1. Astronomy projects—Juvenile literature. [1. Astronomy projects.   2. Astronomy.   3. Science projects.] I. Keen, Dan.
II. Title.
QB64.B64   1991
520′.78—dc20   91-34394
                                                  CIP
                                                   AC

TAB Books offers software for sale. For information and a catalog, please contact TAB Software Department, Blue Ridge Summit, PA 17294-0850.

Acquisitions Editor: Kimberly Tabor
Book Editor: Lori Flaherty
Book Design: Jaclyn J. Boone
Illustrations: Carol Chapin   SFPS

92-1090

Contents

Introduction

More than likely, all of us have been required to do at least one science project during our school years. It might have been growing seeds in kindergarten or building a Tesla Coil in high school. No matter, such experiences are not forgotten and help shape our view of the world around us.

Doing a science project yields many benefits beyond the obvious educational value. The logical processes required help encourage clear, concise thinking, which can carry through a student's entire life. A successful science project can provide a student with the motivation to strive for success in other areas because it requires a disciplined mind, clear notes and data gathering, curiosity and patience, an honesty regarding results and procedures, and a concise reporting of work accomplished.

If you are a parent, we encourage you to work with your child on projects. A science project can foster good communication between your youngster and yourself as well as enhancing your child's self-esteem.

Finally, there is always the possibility of a spin-off interest developing. A youngster who chooses to do a project in mathematics, perhaps using a battery, switches, and light bulbs to represent binary numbers, might discover a liking for electronics.

But where does the student, teacher, or parent find suggestions for science projects? It is our aim to fill this void by offering a large collection of projects and project ideas in the Science Fair Project Series books. So whether you are a teacher who is interested in doing classroom projects, a student assigned a class project, or a parent who wants to help your child with a science fair project, the Science Fair Project Series can help.

Our goal is to provide complete project ideas using valid scientific processes and procedures. Students need a starting place and direction. We have provided that with questions posed in the form of needs or problems (discovering how to get electricity from the Sun was born out of a need, for example). We have also provided overviews, organizational direction, possible hypotheses, materials lists, procedures, and controls. All of the projects explained are complete but can be used as spring boards to create expanded or new projects. All projects contain suggestions for continuing a project further.

Each chapter is organized by topic. Some projects might overlap into more than one science discipline as well as within the discipline. In these cases, we have placed such projects under their dominant theme. Projects are designed for the sixth to ninth grade student. Many projects, however, can be watered down and used for children in lower grades. Similarly, students in higher grades can brainstorm ideas to more advanced levels.

It is very important to read the introduction at the beginning of each chapter from which you plan on doing a project. Information that is relevant to each project is given there. The appendix lists suppliers where laboratory supplies can be purchased.

Once you have selected a project and read the chapter introduction, read the entire project through carefully. This will help you understand the overall scope of the project, the materials needed, the time requirements, and the procedure *before* you begin.

Safety and ethics must be a consideration before beginning any project. Some projects require cutting with a knife or scissors. Use common sense. Projects that must have adult supervision are indicated with the phrase **Adult Supervision Required** next to the title. These projects deal with caustics, poisons, acids, high temperatures, high voltages, or other potentially hazardous conditions. Ethical science concepts involve very careful considerations about living organisms. One cannot recklessly cause pain, damage, or death to any living organism.

There is no limit to the number of themes and the number of hypotheses one can form about our universe. It is as infinite as the stars in the heavens. It is our hope that many students will be creative with the ideas presented here and develop their own unique hypotheses and proceed with their experiments using accepted scientific methods.

Some projects can go on for years. There is no reason to stop a project other than losing interest in it. It might be that what you studied this year can be taken a step further next year. With each question or curiosity answered, more questions are raised—that is the nature of science.

It has been our experience that answers produce new and exciting questions. We believe that science discovery and advancement proceeds as much on excellent questions as it does on excellent answers.

We hope we can stimulate you, your students, or your youngster's imagination and encourage creative thinking. Learning is rewarding and enjoyable. Best of luck with your project.

Robert L. Bonnet
G. Daniel Keen

How to Use This Book

All projects that require adult supervision have the **STOP** symbol at the beginning of the project. No responsibility is implied or taken for anyone who sustains injuries as a result of using the materials or ideas put forward in this book. Taste nothing. Use proper equipment (gloves, safety glasses, and other safety precautions). Clean up broken glass with a dustpan and brush. Use chemicals with extra care. Wash hands after project work is done. Tie up loose hair and clothing. Follow step-by-step procedures; avoid short cuts. Never work alone. Remember, adult supervision is advised. Safety precautions are addressed in the text. If you use common sense and make safety the first consideration, you will create safe, fun, educational, and rewarding projects.

1

Science
Projects

Before beginning work on a science project, there are some important things you need to know. It is important that you read this chapter before starting on a project. It defines terms and sets up guidelines that should be followed as work on the project progresses.

Beginning without Pain

To proceed with a science project, you must first fully understand the term *science project*. Older students are familiar with report writing. Many types of reports are required at all grade levels, whether it be book reports, history reports, or term papers. Although a report might be required to accompany a science project, it is not the focal point. The body of science comes from experimentation. Most projects discover information by scientific methods, or a formal approach to scientific investigation. It is a step-by-step, logical thinking process that can be grouped into four sections:

1. The statement of the problem.

2. The hypothesis.

3. Experimentation and information gathering (results).

4. A conclusion based on the hypothesis.

In science, a statement of the "problem" does not necessarily mean that something went wrong. A problem is something for which there is no good answer. Air pollution is a problem. Aggressive behavior, crab grass, and obesity are problems. Any question can be stated as a problem.

Once you think of a problem, discuss your ideas with someone else—a friend, teacher, parent, or someone working in the field you are investigating. Find out what has already been done on the subject and if the scope of your project is appropriate.

A hypothesis is an educated guess. It is educated because you have knowledge about trees, dogs, or whatever the subject matter may be. Your life experiences help you form a specific hypothesis rather than a random one. Suppose you hypothesize, "If I add sugar to water and feed it to this plant, it will grow better." A "control" plant would be needed, namely, a plant that was given only water. Both plants would be given the identical amount of Sunshine, water, temperature, and any other nonexperimental factors.

Assumptions

Any assumption in science must be specifically defined. What is meant by saying "The plant will grow better"? What is "better" assumed to be? Does it mean greener leaves, faster growing, bigger foliage, better tasting fruit, more kernels per cob?

If you are growing plants from seeds, the assumption is made that all the seeds are of equal quality. When several plants are used in an experiment, it is assumed that all the plants are the same at the start of the project.

Before beginning a project, be sure to state all your assumptions. If the results of an experiment are challenged, the challenge should be on the assumptions and not on the procedure.

Sample Size

Sample size refers to the number of items in a test. The larger the sample size, the more significant the results. Using only two plants to test the sugar theory would not yield a lot of confidence in the results. One plant might have grown better than the other because some plants just grow better than others. Obviously, your statistical data becomes more meaningful when you sample a larger group of items in an experiment. As the group size increases, individual differences become less important.

Measurements

Making accurate measurements is a must. The experimenter must report the truth, and not let bias (his or her feelings) affect his measurements. As mentioned earlier, the reason science progresses is because we do not have to reinvent the wheel. Science knowledge builds on what people have proven before us. It is important to document (record) the results. They must be replicable (able to be repeated), so others can duplicate our efforts. Good controls, procedures, and clear recordkeeping are essential. As information is gathered, the results may lead to further investigation or raise more questions that need asking.

Conclusions

The conclusion of an experiment must be related to the hypothesis. Was the hypothesis correct or incorrect? Perhaps it was correct in one aspect but not in another. In the sugar example, adding sugar to the water might have helped, but only to a point. The human body can use a certain amount of sugar for energy, but too much could cause obesity.

There is no failure in a science experiment. The hypothesis might be proven wrong but something was learned from the experience. Information has been gained. Many experiments prove to be of seemingly no value except that someone reading the results will not have to spend the time repeating the same experiment. That is why it is important to thoroughly report results. Mankind's knowledge builds on past successes *and* failures.

Collections, Demonstrations, and Models

Competitive science fairs usually require experimentation. Collections and models by themselves are not experiments, although they can be turned into experiments. A collection is gathered data. Suppose a collection of shells has been assembled from along the eastern seaboard of the United States. The structure and composition of shells from the south can be compared to those found in the north. Then the collection becomes more experimental. Similarly, an insect collection can deal with insect physiology or comparative anatomy. A rock and mineral collection might indicate a greater supply of one type of rock or mineral over another because of the geology of the area from which it was collected. Leaves could be gathered from trees to survey the available species of trees in your area.

Classroom assignments that use demonstrations or models can help students better understand scientific concepts. A steam engine dramatically shows how heat is converted to steam and steam is converted into mechanical energy. Seeing it happen could have greater educational impact than merely talking about it.

Individuals Versus Group Projects

A teacher might require a group of students to work on a project. Groups are difficult for a teacher to evaluate. Who did the most work? If, however, it is being dealt with on an interest level, then the more help received, the better the project might be. Individual versus group projects bear directly on the intended goal. Keep in mind, however, that most science fairs do not accept group projects.

Choosing a Topic

Select a topic of interest; something that arouses curiosity. One only needs to look through a newspaper to find a contemporary topic: dolphins washing up on the beach, the effect of the ozone layer on plants, stream erosion.

Limitations and Precautions

Of course, safety must always be placed first when doing a project. Using voltages higher than those found in batteries can cause electrical shock. Poisons, acids, and caustics must be carefully monitored by an adult. Temperature extremes, both hot and cold, can cause harm. Sharp objects or objects that can shatter, such as glass, can be dangerous. Nothing in chemistry should be tasted. Some combinations of chemicals can produce toxic materials. Safety goggles, aprons, heat gloves, rubber gloves for caustics and acids, vented hoods, and adult supervision are just some safety considerations. Each project should be evaluated for the need of these various safety materials.

Projects in this book that require an adult to supervise you are indicated as such in the project title. Finally, special considerations should be considered if a project is to be left unattended and accessible to the public.

Most science fairs have ethical rules and guidelines for live animals, especially vertebrates, which are given thoughtful consideration. In some cases, you could be required to present a note from a veterinarian or other professional that states that training with the animal has been dealt with. Perhaps your experiment calls for using mice to run through a maze to demonstrate learning or behavior.

Limitations on time, help, and money are also important factors. How much money will or should be spent should be addressed by a science fair committee. Generally, when a project is entered in a science fair, the more money spent on the display, the better the chance of winning. It isn't fair that one child might only have $1.87 to spend on a project while another might have $250. Unfortunately, the packaging does influence the judging at many science fairs. An additional problem might be that one student's parent is a science teacher and another student's parent might be unavailable or unable to help.

Science Fair Judging

In general, science fairs lack well-defined standards. The criteria for evaluation can vary from school to school, area to area, and region to region. Therefore, we would like to propose some goals for students and teachers to consider when judging.

A truly good science project should be one that requires creative thinking and investigation by the student. Recordkeeping, logical sequence, presentation, and originality are important points.

The thoroughness of a student's project reflects the background work that was done. If the student is present, a judge might orally quiz the experimenter to see if he or she has sufficient understanding of the subject. Recording all experiences, such as talking to someone knowledgeable in the subject or reading material on it, will show the amount of research put into the project. Consequently, teachers should urge students to keep a record of all the time they spend on a project. Clarity of the problem, assumptions, procedures, observations, and conclusions are important judging criteria as well. Be specific.

Points should be given for skill. Skills could be in computation, laboratory work, observation, measurement, construction, and the like. Technical ability and workmanship are necessary to a good project.

Often, projects with flashier display boards do better. Some value should be placed on dramatic presentation but it should not outweigh other important criteria, such as originality. Graphs, tables, and other illustrations can be good visual aids to the interpretation of data. Photographs are especially important for projects where it is impossible to set the project up indoors (a fairy ring in the forest, for example).

Some science fairs might require a short abstract or synopsis in logical sequence. If this is the case, be sure it includes the purpose, assumptions, a hypothesis, materials, procedures, and conclusion.

Competing

Often, a project will compete with others, whether it is at the class level or at a science fair. Find out ahead of time what the rules are for the competition. Check to see if there is a limit on project size. Will an accompanying research paper be required? Will it have to be orally defended? Will the exhibit have to be left unattended overnight? Leaving a $3,000 computer unattended overnight would be a big risk.

Find out which category has the greatest competition. You may be up against less competition by placing your project in another category. If it is a "crossover" project, you may wish to place it in a category that has fewer entries. For example, a project that deals with chloroplasts could be classified under botany or chemistry. A project dealing with the wavelength of light hitting a plant could be botany or physics.

Space and Astronomy

This book deals with a wide range of ideas in space and astronomy. A few projects are demonstrations because, currently, only astronauts can go into space to perform science projects. But most are experimental, because upper-level science fairs traditionally require projects to state a hypothesis and then set out to experimentally prove or disprove that hypothesis. Photography and computers are used by modern astronomers, and several projects in this book incorporate these tools. Not everyone has a telescope, therefore, many projects suggested do not require the use of one.

Observers have been awed by the night sky for centuries. The excitement of astronomy has been passed from generation to generation. Hopefully, some of you will carry this knowledge, wisdom, and excitement into future generations.

2

Observing the Heavens

With our busy daily schedules, few of us are as familiar with the skies as our ancestors. How peaceful it is to lay on the ground on a quiet night and look up at the grandeur of the heavens. We know much more about the heavens than early man but our desire to learn more is never-ending, and observers never cease to marvel at its wonders. We had romantic notions about the Moon in the early 1930s and 1940s, then we later put our feet on it. It is no longer fairy tales. It is now the reality of science. The mystery and fear have given way to knowledge. Some of our wonder is lost but some is enhanced.

PROJECT 2-1
Closer to Brighter

Overview

The pinpoints of starlight in the night sky vary from distinct brilliance to barely able to be seen. Astronomers measure this apparent brightness of stars with a scale called "magnitude." Some stars appear brighter than others because they give off more light. Some seem brighter to us because they are closer, not because they really give off more light. Hypothesize that you can position a weak flashlight and a strong flashlight at various distances from an observer to fool the observer into thinking both light sources are of equal brightness.

Materials

- 2 identical flashlights
- weak set of flashlight batteries
- strong set of flashlight batteries
- 2 orange crates or plastic milk cartons
- several friends or family members to be observers
- logbook and pencil

Procedure

Conduct this experiment on a dark night when the Moon is not bright. The area should be fairly dark, such as a rural area away from lighted buildings and street lights.

Place a flashlight with fresh batteries on an orange crate, plastic milk carton, or cardboard box. It must be tall enough to lift the flashlight a few feet off the ground. Put the flashlight and box far away from the area where you plan to have your observers stand. Put a flashlight with weaker batteries on a box and move it much closer.

Try different locations for the two flashlights. When you believe you have placed them in such a way that the light from both of them appears to be equal in brightness, you are ready to test your hypothesis by bringing observers to your observation spot.

Independently have one observer at a time cover one of his or her eyes with one hand and look toward the two flashlights. One eye is covered to avoid depth perception, which might cause the observer to realize which light is closer. Ask the observer whether the two lights are equal in brightness or if one is brighter than the other. If the observer believes one is brighter, ask which one. Keep a log of the responses of each observer. Study your results, and reach a conclusion regarding your hypothesis.

Going Further

1. Using a camera, open the shutter for varying lengths of time. How does time exposures compare to the opinions of naked-eye observations?

2. Put various types of lenses in front of the lights to change the distance at which it seems brighter.

3. Research the five nearest stars and the five largest stars in the night sky. Compare their brightness (in magnitude). How does their size relate to their distance from the Earth? Are there other factors to consider?

4. What are the brightest objects in the night sky? Venus is the brightest object other than the Moon or an occasional phenomena such as a meteor. Does the light reflected from Venus increase or decrease due to its orbital position or ours?

PROJECT 2-2
Heat Wave
Adult Supervision Required

Overview

When we stargaze on a crisp, clear night, it is easy to forget that we are actually looking through miles of atmosphere. Water vapor, dust particles, gases, and other obstacles fill the air. Heated air can strongly interfere with our visual observations too. Most people are familiar with road mirages. The hot Sun beats on the road surface warming the air above it, causing it to reflect the sky above. This gives the appearance of a distant pool of water.

For successful telescope observing, it is important that the telescope not be aimed through any Earthly sources of heat, such as rising heat from chimneys and smokestacks or even heat radiated from the roof of your house.

Hypothesize that you must avoid any heat sources near your viewing area or the objects viewed through a telescope will be distorted.

Materials

- telescope
- roof-top chimney with a fire in a fireplace or a woodstove that is burning

Procedure

Locate a house (yours or a friends) that has a chimney or stove pipe on the roof. Have an adult light a fire in the fireplace. Outside, focus the telescope on an object that is in the path of the heat rising from the chimney (Fig. 2-1). This experiment can be conducted at night with the telescope focused on a star. It could also be done in the day, pointing the telescope toward other objects (bird, mountain, skyscraper) or other object in the distance through the chimney heat. Assuming it is conducted at night, the star viewed through the telescope will appear to be distorted, wavering and shimmering.

Next, move the telescope to another area in the yard where the same star (or object) can be viewed without being in direct line of the chimney. Does the object now appear steady? Was your hypothesis correct?

Fig. 2-1. *Looking through heated air will cause distortion.*

Going Further

Can this technique be used to detect areas of heat loss in your home? On a cold evening does heat radiate from your roof, doors, and windows? Is heat lost through your chimney even when there is no fire going?

PROJECT 2-3
So Far Away

Overview

When working with the concepts of astronomy, it is necessary to deal with large numbers. Speeds, distances, sizes, weights, and densities are often huge figures, running into the millions, billions, and beyond. The average distance between the Earth and the Sun is 93 million miles. The human mind cannot easily conceptualize such an enormous distance.

Hypothesize that you can help the average person get a better understanding of many gigantic astronomical terms by representing them in more familiar terms.

Materials

- research materials
- calculator, paper, and pencil
- arts and crafts materials (glue, construction paper, scissors)
- observers: friends, relatives, or fellow students

Procedure

This project requires some artwork to enhance the display and to present the representations. First, research some of the more common astronomically used figures. Make analogies (comparisons) of them to everyday common objects and times. Show the relationship graphically in your display. For example, we said that the Sun is 93 million miles away. Give people a better understanding of this distance by drawing a car leaving the Sun and traveling 60 miles per hour on a straight line toward the Earth. This trip would take about 176 years (Fig. 2-2). Some other suggestions:

- The Sun is one astronomical unit (1 AU) from the Earth.
- A person standing at the equator is moving 1,000 miles per hour as the Earth rotates.
- Traveling at the speed of light, 186,000 miles per second, it takes a radio message sent from Earth four years, four months, and seven days to reach the nearest star (other than our Sun).
- Mercury, the swiftest moving planet, is the smallest. Represent its size compared to all the planets by relating it to a grain of sand, vegetables (like peas), and fruit.
- Compare planet densities. Although Saturn is many times

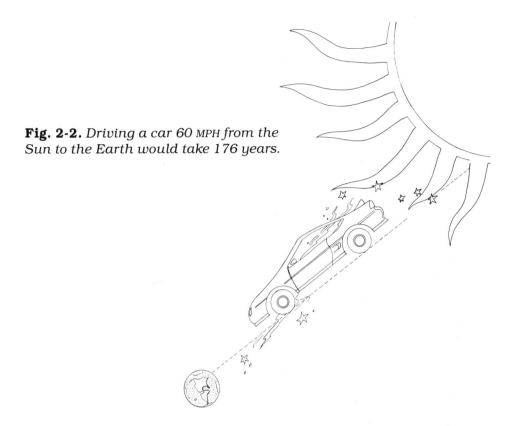

Fig. 2-2. *Driving a car 60 MPH from the Sun to the Earth would take 176 years.*

bigger than the Earth, its density is so light that a piece of it would float in water.

- Compare planet gravities. If you can jump five feet high on Earth, you can jump 18 feet high on Mercury but only two feet on Jupiter.

After constructing your display, have your friends, teachers, relatives, and fellow students examine it. Ask them if your display gives them a better comprehension of the astronomical figures you portray. To avoid biased answers, make a pretest for them to take, show them your display, and then test them again. Reach a conclusion about your hypothesis.

PROJECT 2-4
Now You See It, Now You Don't
Adult Supervision Required

Overview

Occulation is when one astronomical body passes between the Earth and another astronomical body that appears smaller. The larger body is said to "occult," or block our view of the smaller body. The most common occurrence of occulations are caused by the Moon. Occulations are of scientific interest for several reasons. If the Moon is involved, scientists can get a direct measurement of the outline edge of the Moon. When a star is occulted, the star's size can be measured by special electronic equipment.

Hypothesize that occulations can be used to detect an astronomical body that we cannot see, such as a black hole that doesn't emit (give off) light. Construct a working model to demonstrate.

Materials

- cardboard box at least 2′ on any given side
- flat, black spray paint
- 1- or 2″-diameter Styrofoam ball
- black thread
- utility knife (**caution: very sharp tool**)
- adhesive tape or glue
- electronic hookup wire (thin gauge solid strand is best)
- black electrical tape
- 1$\frac{1}{2}$-volt flashlight battery and holder
- LED (light emitting diode)—available at Radio Shack
- optional: solder gun or solder pencil (**caution: solder guns get very hot**)

Procedure

It is best to have the cardboard box as deep as possible. Spray paint the inside of the box black. Also, spray paint a small Styrofoam ball with flat, black paint. Using a utility knife or an awl, have an adult cut a small opening in the center of one of the sides of the box, just big enough to allow the eye of an observer to peer into the box.

At the end of the box opposite the peep hole, cut a tiny hole and insert a small LED so that the bulb will shine inside the box. Glue or tape it to keep it from falling out. Use hookup wire and a battery to power the light.

Perpendicular to the peep hole, cut a small, half-inch-wide slot all the way across the top of the box. Tie a piece of three-foot-long thread to the Styrofoam ball. Place the ball at the bottom of the box and feed the free end of the thread up through the slot. Tape the top of the box shut. You should be able to move the styrofoam ball around the inside of the box, much like a marionette. The constructed box is shown in Fig. 2-3.

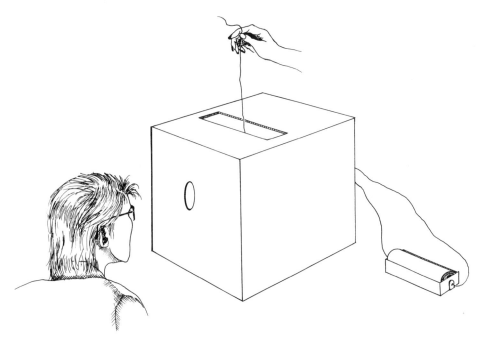

Fig. 2-3. *Construct a box to demonstrate occulation.*

In a dark room, have an observer look through the peep hole and view the lit bulb, which represents a star. The LED should not give off enough light to allow the observer to see the Styrofoam ball.

The ball represents a dark astronomical body, perhaps a black hole or other phenomena that does not emit any light. Slowly move the ball around until the observer views an occulation of the LED.

PROJECT 2-5

Balancing Act

Adult Supervision Required

Overview

The gravitational attraction of two masses as close together as the Earth and Moon, causes them to orbit around a point that is the center of the masses. Actually, the Moon doesn't simply orbit the Earth but rather they are both orbiting around the *barycenter*, or the center balancing point of the system. Figure 2-4 shows the barycenter of a typical system containing a large mass and a small one. Surprisingly, the barycenter for the Earth and Moon is slightly inside the Earth, because the Earth has so much more mass.

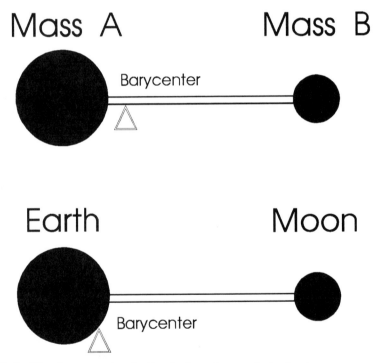

Fig. 2-4. *The barycenter is the balancing point of a two-mass system.*

Hypothesize that the barycenter of a two-mass system can be located and identified. With the device you will construct, you can show individuals who would typically think that the center of gravity for the Earth and Moon would be close to the Earth, that the center is actually inside the larger mass.

Materials

- 2″-diameter Styrofoam ball
- 8″-diameter Styrofoam ball
- 1″ × 20″ × 3″ piece of wood
- 2 1″ × 12″ × 3″ piece of wood
- 1/4″ × 3′ piece of wood (dowel)
- 1 or 2 1½″-long finishing nails
- hammer

Procedure

Push an 8-inch-diameter Styrofoam ball onto the 1/4-inch wooden dowel. Position it at the center of the dowel. Because equal amounts of the dowel extend on both sides of the ball, the assumption is that the mass of the dowel is balanced and, therefore, not a factor in the two-mass system. Push a 2-inch-diameter Styrofoam ball onto one end of the dowel.

Next, you want to determine the balancing point of the system (the barycenter). You will show that the center point is actually inside the larger ball by locating the balancing point on the ball. Normally, a single point is used to balance, but to give your system more stability, you will rest the ball on two nails and use two side panels by the small ball to minimize lateral (sideways) motion.

Have an adult cut the lengths of wood specified in the materials list. At one end of the 20-inch-long 1-by-3-inch board, hammer two finishing nails into the board just deep enough to be secure. The nails should be about 2 inches apart. With finishing nails, construct the side panels on the board, opposite the end with the finishing nails. See Fig. 2-5.

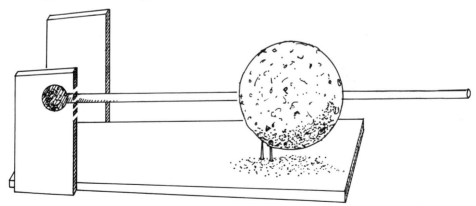

Fig. 2-5. *The barycenter for the Earth/Moon system is actually inside the Earth.*

Locate the barycenter on your system by moving the 8-inch Styrofoam ball on the nails, balancing it.

Going Further

1. Call the system a binary (something made of two things or parts) star system.

2. Instead of balancing on a fulcrum (support) point underneath, hang it like a mobile, locating the point on the sphere where the system balances.

3. Cut a triangle shape out of a piece of light plywood. Experiment placing different weights (use clay) at each apex (angle) and determine the balance point. Balance by hammering a nail slightly into a piece of wood to act as a fulcrum.

PROJECT 2-6
Spotting the Sun
Adult Supervision Required

Overview

NEVER LOOK DIRECTLY AT THE SUN. NEVER LOOK DIRECTLY AT THE SUN THROUGH A TELESCOPE, BINOCULARS, OR ANY OTHER DEVICE.

The Sun may seem to be an unblemished burning ball, but on closer inspection, dark spots, or sunspots, can often be seen on its surface. Astronomers can view the Sun through telescopes by using special filters to reduce the light to a safe level.

Sunspots are caused by lower temperature areas. They really aren't black (they are still shining brightly), but they appear dark against the bright background.

Hypothesize that the Sun's surface is not unblemished but is marred by dark spots.

Materials

- cardboard box (shoe box size or larger—the larger the better)
- utility knife
- 2 unruled, white index cards
- tape
- straight pin
- Sunny day

Procedure

To safely view the Sun, construct an observation box as shown in Fig. 2-6. Have an adult cut the flaps off of a cardboard box and discard them. Stand the box upright so that the open side faces you. The box should stand taller than it is wide. Tape a plain white index card to the bottom inside of the box. At the top, have an adult cut a 2-by-2-inch square. Tape a stiff piece of very thin cardboard, such as oak tag, another index card, or an unwanted greeting card, over the 2-by-2-inch gap. Stick a pin through the center of the card, making a small, perfectly round hole. This pinhole box arrangement is similar to the old "pinhole camera" concept (research how a pinhole camera works). Light travels in a straight line, as shown, forming an image of the Sun at the bottom of the box.

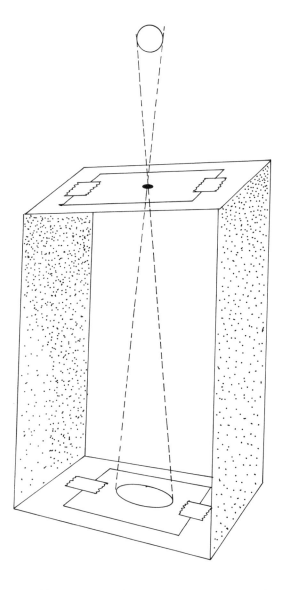

Fig. 2-6. *Construct a box for safely viewing the sun.*

Point your Sun viewer toward the Sun. A small image of the Sun will appear on the index card inside the box. You might have to move the index card closer or farther away from the pinhole to focus the image. The image can be enlarged by using a bigger box. Can you detect any spots on the Sun?

Going Further

1. To get a bigger and sharper image of the Sun, use a telescope or binoculars to focus the Sun's image onto an index card (**do not**

look through the telescope or binoculars directly). Do not do this for any length of time or it can damage lenses.

2. Follow the sunspots over a period of time, sketching the patterns they form. Compare them from one Monday to the next Monday.

PROJECT 2-7
Big Moon, Little Moon

Overview

We can't always trust what we see. Our mind and our eyes can play tricks on us when we view the Moon on the horizon. At times, when the Moon is near the horizon, the brain tends to perceive it as though it were at the distance of the horizon. The Moon falsely appears to be bigger when it is at the horizon than when it is viewed overhead.

Hypothesize that you can prove the eyes and mind can unconsciously give us false information about the size of an object. It is important that individuals are aware of such phenomena.

Materials

- arts and crafts materials (glue, markers, construction paper, scissors, etc.)
- observers
- logbook

Procedure

Using arts and crafts materials, create a large pictorial display as shown in Fig. 2-7. Have several dozen friends, teachers, parents, neighbors, and fellow students view your display. Ask them which of the two discs in the picture appears bigger, the one closest to the foreground or the one on the distant horizon. Tell the observers that it is not important which disc is larger or smaller, simply that they tell which one "appears" biggest to them. Record their responses in a logbook and use this data to reach a conclusion about your hypothesis.

Going Further

1. Build an optical illusion that would cause confusion in the mind concerning distance. Use different size objects to create the illusion of distance. Would eye dominance (left eye, right eye) cause a difference?

2. Is the horizon more significant or the vanishing point?

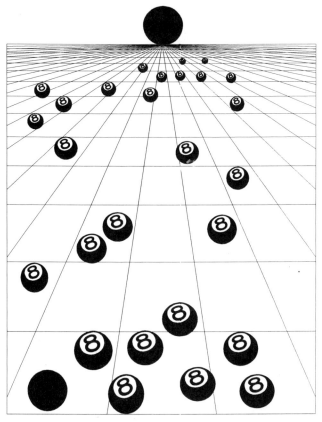

Fig. 2-7. *An optical illusion results when the brain perceives an object close to the horizon as being larger than an equal-sized object that is closer.*

PROJECT 2-8
Focus In

Overview

When looking through a telescope or a lens to make distant objects appear closer, the gain in magnification causes a decrease in the field of vision. We define "field of vision" as the width of the opening you can see. For example, you can see the whole Moon when you look at it with your naked eye. If you look at the Moon through a telescope, you can see it in much greater detail but you cannot see all of the Moon's surface at the same time.

Hypothesize that, as magnification with a lens increases, the field of vision decreases.

Materials

- binoculars
- meter or yardstick
- tape
- logbook
- camera and film

Procedure

Tape a meter or yardstick securely on a wall. Have an adult choose the wall, because they will know which wall in your home will not be marred by the temporary use of tape. The meter stick can be mounted either horizontally or vertically. Positioning a meter stick does not matter because you are looking through a round lens and so the diameter in view will be equal, whether horizontal or vertical.

Stand 10 feet away from the wall that has the yardstick taped on it. You will be able to see the entire yardstick using your naked eye. Look through a pair of binoculars. You can use a camera with a telephoto lens. Pictures make a nice addition to your display board.

Read and calculate the number of inches that you can see in the eye piece. You may opt to position the ruler at zero on one side of the eye piece as a starting point. Record that number. Use the logbook to record the width in inches seen in your field of view as you move closer and as you move further away. Reach a conclusion about your hypothesis.

Going Further

1. Knowing the magnification power of the binoculars, create a relationship between the power, the distances viewed, and the number of meters (or other appropriate measure) in the field of view.

2. Can the focus adjustment wheel on binoculars be used to determine distance by focusing on different objects at different wheel positions?

PROJECT 2-9
Bigger Is Not Better

Overview

While lenses can increase our ability to see distant objects in greater detail, they can introduce distortions of the object. It is important for astronomers to know and understand lens distortions so they can compensate for them. Increasing magnification can compound or increase distortion.

Hypothesize that magnification is not the key to viewing distant objects in astronomy. It does not matter how big you can make an object appear if that object is blurry or distorted. You cannot multiply lenses to achieve unlimited magnification. For this reason, astronomers try to get the largest single lens or mirror reflector they can (larger telescopes also gather more light through larger openings).

Materials

- 2 magnifying glasses
- binoculars
- telescope
- sheet of graph paper, 8½″ × 11″
- cardboard box equal to, or larger than, 8½″ × 11″
- tape

Procedure

Tape a sheet of graph paper onto the side of a cardboard box or other support to stand it up vertically. Hold a magnifying glass a few inches in front of the graph paper. Now hold another magnifying glass between your eye and the first magnifying glass. Does this double magnification make the graph paper appear even more magnified? Does it distort the paper? Are the lines on the graph paper still straight or are they distorted?

Look at a distant object through a pair of binoculars. What happens when a magnifying glass is placed in front of (or behind) the binoculars? Similarly, put a magnifying glass in line with a telescope. Remember, **never look directly at the Sun. Never look directly at the Sun through a telescope, binoculars, or any other device.**

Going Further

1. Research other types of distortion or "aberration." For example, color distortions through a lens or distortions due to distance.

2. What is focal length? Will the focal length determine the distance between the magnifying objects?

PROJECT 2-10
Comparative: Magnitude

Overview

The relative brightness of the stars is called *magnitude*. Astronomers today use photometers and telescopes to accurately measure magnitude. This field of study is called astronomical photometry. But Hipparchus, a Greek astronomer, categorized the brightness of the stars that could be seen with the naked eye over 2,000 years ago, long before the invention of the telescope. He assigned each star that could be observed a number from one to six, representing the brightest to the dimmest.

Hypothesize that with the naked eye you can categorize relative brightness of stars and do it with an accuracy that is close to the measured magnitude.

Materials

- star chart
- logbook
- research materials

Procedure

Use a star chart to identify the stars in the evening sky. In a logbook, write the name of several dozens stars that you can identify. Pick a sampling of stars that run the range of the brightest to the dimmest. Study the various brightness of the stars you see. In your log, assign each star a number from one to six, from brightest to dimmest.

Research the magnitude of the stars you categorized. Compare their magnitude as measured by astronomers to the brightness relationship you found. Is the brightness relationship you assigned to the stars similar to the astronomers' measured results? Reach a conclusion about your hypothesis.

Going Further

1. Use the stars in three constellations (gathering or grouping) that you can easily identify and look up.

2. Set up a magnitude scale for the planets. If you wish to compare a planet that you can't see, such as a morning star that can't be seen while viewing another, find a star of similar brightness, one which is there all the time.

3

Clocks,
Calendars,
and Time

For thousands of years, mankind has used the rotating Earth as a master clock, even before it was realized that the Earth was round and was rotating. Our clocks and calendars are based on the movements of the Sun and planets. The period of time that passes in order for the Earth to make one complete revolution on its axis is the basis of our clock system. Timekeeping is very important to each one of us. Our lives are wrapped around daily time schedules. This chapter deals with calendars and time, topics that are especially important in the field of astronomy.

PROJECT 3-1
Right Place, Wrong Time

Overview

The sundial was one of the earliest known devices for breaking a day down into smaller parts (hours). On a sundial, time is determined by measuring the shadow of a vertically standing object called the *gnomon* or *style*. As the Sun moves across the sky (east to west) from sunrise until sunset, the shadow cast by the gnomon moves from one side to the other. But if a sundial is set up so that the gnomon's shadow falls correctly on an hour mark on one day of the year, the actual time will be a little later or earlier for other days of the year.

Two variables come into play that cause the sundial's shadow not to fall exactly on the right mark all year. First, the Earth travels faster in its orbit when it gets closest to the Sun. Second, the distance between the Sun and the Earth changes through the course of a year. The reason for these two occurrences is because the Earth's orbit is elliptical (oval) in shape rather than a perfect circle.

Hypothesize that the gnomon's shadow does not fall exactly on the correct hour markings on a sundial each day of the year because of the Sun's irregular movement as it travels across the sky. This project requires a minimum of two months to gather sufficient data.

Note: Although the sundial might seem to be in error, it gives amazingly accurate time by reading the dial and then adding or subtracting a known corrective number of minutes for the given day of the year. Tables showing the number of minutes to add or subtract are commonly given in books on sundials. This table is called "The Equation of Time." The Equation of Time is the difference between the reading of the sundial and the reading of a uniformly running clock ticking off 24 hours per day.

Materials

- round, wooden dowel about 1/2" in diameter × 5"
- 1 SF of plywood
- 1"-long, flat head wood screw
- marking pen
- pencil and logbook
- accurate clock
- accurate time source to set the clock, such as the WWV

radio station found on shortwave radio, desktop weather/time radios, or the telephone company

Procedure

Construct a sundial by securing a short, vertically standing wooden dowel to a piece of plywood. This can be done by using a screw piercing up through the bottom of the plywood and screwing the dowel down onto it. Have an adult drill or cut the wood. You might opt to use a garden, if you have one available, rather than constructing one.

Find a spot in your yard that gets full sunshine during the day and does not have any shadows cast by trees, the house, or other structures. Place the sundial in this area. It is important that the sundial does not move over the length of time you will be conducting your experiment (spanning several months). It must be secured from movement.

Readings Done When The Sundial Shadow Exactly Points To 8AM

Date	Actual Clock Time	Difference + or - Minutes

Fig. 3-1. *Chart for logging sundial readings.*

Set up a logbook as shown in the example in Fig. 3-1. Each day when the time shown on the sundial reads 8:00 A.M., for example, check the real time on a clock. Record the difference in the number of minutes. Part of the year, the sundial will be ahead, and during other times, it will be behind. Cloudy days will have to be left blank on the log sheet but it is only necessary to obtain a few readings a week to determine the trend for a period of time or several months. After gathering data for at least two months, reach a conclusion about your hypothesis.

Going Further

1. Use the data you have collected to plot a chart on graph paper that visually demonstrates the difference between the sundial indication and the clock.

2. If the gnomon is pointed precisely to the celestial pole, the shadow cast shows the correct solar time. Properly align a sundial and check it daily against an accurate clock. Write the discrepency in minutes between the Sundial and the clock. After one year, create a table for the Equation of Time.

3. The Moon follows the path of the Sun across the sky fairly closely. Use the Moon's shadow to establish a "moondial" for determining the hour at night.

4. What would be the best day of the year to set your sundial, and why?

PROJECT 3-2
Skipping a Leap

Overview

The calendar, our way of keeping track of months, days, and years, is based on the Earth's relationship to the Sun. The year is broken into smaller parts, months, which are based on the way the Moon appears in the sky. The invention of the calendar to measure time was a great achievement. Growing crops could now be more effective.

Early calendars were inaccurate and often laid out in a confusing manner, however. Some order to the calendar can be attributed to Julius Caesar, who devised the idea of adding an extra day every four years because the 365 day calendar was slightly inaccurate. But by the sixteenth century, the vernal equinox (the day on which there is an equal amount of sunlight and darkness) was occurring on March 11 instead of March 21. This is because a day is really 11 minutes and 15 seconds longer than 356 1/4 days per year. So, Pope Gregory XIII issued an edict setting up the schedule we use today, where centuries are not considered to be leap years unless they are divisible by 400. Therefore, the years 1700, 1800, and 1900 were not leap years, but the year 2000 will be.

Hypothesize that you can write a computer program that will determine if a year will be a leap year, based on the calendar formula we use today. Note that this project could also be placed under math or computer categories in a science fair.

Materials

- computer
- understanding of a computer language

Procedure

Write a computer program in which a user can enter a year and the computer will determine if that year will be a leap year or not. Figure 3-2 shows one suggestion for writing the program in the BASIC language. "Dress up" your program to include attractive screen displays and "idiot proof" the input so that a person cannot type in a foolish entry for the year (a negative number for example).

Going Further

1. Write the program in several computer languages and make comparisons.

```
10 REM    ***********************
20 REM    *  Leap Year Program  *
30 REM    ***********************
40 PRINT "Enter the year (YYYY): ";
50 INPUT YEAR
60 IF YEAR/4 = INT(YEAR/4) THEN 90
70 PRINT "The year ";YEAR;" is not a leap year."
80 GOTO 140
90 IF YEAR/100 = INT(YEAR/100) THEN 120
100 PRINT "The year ";YEAR;" is a leap year."
110 GOTO 140
120 IF YEAR/400 <> INT(YEAR/400) THEN 70
130 PRINT "The year ";YEAR;" is a leap year."
140 END
```
Fig. 3-2. *Computer program for calculating leap year.*

2. Research dates and their historical significance. Research local significance. For example, take a school class as a sample and hypothesize that students get higher grades on tests given on Monday than those given on Friday.

3. Assuming the solar year is 365 days, 5 hours, 48 minutes, and 45.7 seconds long, how long will it be before our calendar is in error by one whole day? How much does the Earth slow in its rotation?

4. The Moon's distance from the Earth is increasing 4 centimeters a year. How long will it be before there is a significant effect on the Earth?

PROJECT 3-3
Inconsistent Change

Overview

People often say the days are shorter in the winter and longer in the summer. Of course, all days are equal in length, but this saying is referring to the length of daylight. Because the Earth is tilted on its axis, the Northern Hemisphere faces the Sun during summer and faces away from the Sun during winter. On June 21 (or June 22 depending on the year), the Northern Hemisphere is fully tilted toward the Sun, and the amount of daylight hours is the longest of the year. As the Earth continues its orbit around the Sun, the length of daylight begins to shorten again, until it reaches the day that has the least amount of sunlight on December 21 or 22. These days are called the summer solstice and winter solstice.

In its trek from the "shortest" day to the "longest" and back again, there are obviously two days when the number of daylight hours equals the number of dark hours. These equal days are called the spring equinox, which occurs on March 21 or 22, and the fall equinox, on September 22 or 23.

Does the length of daylight shorten (or lengthen) by an equal amount each day? For example, are there two minutes of extra daylight added each day from the winter solstice to the spring equinox or does the time vary? Hypothesize that the daily change in the amount of daylight will be consistent or inconsistent between a solstice and an equinox or vice versa.

If you hypothesize inconsistent lengths, you might base your prediction on the fact that the Earth's orbit is more of an ellipse than a circle, and the Earth will be closer to the Sun at some times. You might believe that the orbit is close enough to a circle that there would not be any appreciable difference, and therefore, the time is consistent for all practical purposes.

Note that this project should be conducted for at least three months.

Materials

- daily newspaper or television broadcast to gather the daily sunrise and sunset times each day
- logbook

Date	Time Of Sunrise	Time Of Sunset	Amount Of Daylight

Fig. 3-3. *Chart for determining length of day.*

Procedure

Create a log chart with columns set up for recording date, time of sunrise, time of sunset, and amount of daylight as shown in Fig. 3-3. Begin this project on the date of either a solstice or an equinox. These dates were given in the Overview. Conduct the experiment for at least three months to ensure that both an equinox day and a solstice day are part of the data gathered.

Record the time of sunrise and the time of sunset each day. These times are usually listed in the daily newspaper. Calculate the number of hours and minutes of daylight (subtract the sunrise time from the sunset time) and record it. At the end of three months, examine your data and reach a conclusion about your hypothesis.

Going Further

1. Conduct your project over an entire year.

2. Use an almanac to research daylight hours over the past year.

3. Would sunrise times change consistently each day but sunset times vary?

PROJECT 3-4
The Sands of Time
Adult Supervision Required

Overview

Before the invention of mechanical clocks, people devised many ingenius devices for measuring time. The Sun, Moon, stars, and tides were used to mark long passages of time. Shorter time periods were measured by marks on a burning candle or passing a known quantity of sand through a restricted opening in a glass bulb. Large glass bulbs (hour glasses) were used to mark the passage of an hour. Short ones (three minute timers) were used to time boiling eggs.

Hypothesize that you can construct a device out of throwaway materials that can measure a period of time accurately, to within plus or minus one second per minute.

Materials

- two-liter plastic soda bottle
- plastic gallon milk jug
- cork whose diameter is sized to fit snugly into the neck of the soda bottle
- fine sand
- soil sieves or a piece of fine mesh screen
- bucket
- funnel
- drill
- scissors or a utility knife

Procedure

Have an adult drill a small hole ($1/8$ inch or less) all the way through the cork, from top to bottom. The cork must be sized so that it fits into the neck of a two-liter plastic soda bottle.

Collect a bucket of the finest sand you can find. Use a soil sieve or piece of screen to filter out any sand particles that are too big to fit easily through the hole in the cork. It is important that no particles jam in the hole or restrict the flow of the sand.

Using the funnel, pour the sifted sand into a two-liter soda bottle, filling it. Be sure the bottle is dry inside before pouring sand in it. Place the cork in the bottle neck opening. The soda bottle will be placed into the neck of the milk jug. The lip on some milk jugs curves inward enough to prevent the soda bottle from seating down into it. This can be corrected by having an adult cut the top 1/4 inch off the milk jug with a pair of scissors or a utility knife.

Place the sand-filled two-liter bottle into the neck of the milk jug and begin timing as the sand particles flow (Fig. 3-4). Use a stopwatch or clock with a sweep second hand. When the sand looks like it is about to run out, stop it on the nearest minute. The sand now collected in the milk jug will represent a whole number of minutes.

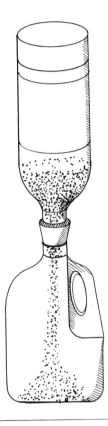

Fig. 3-4. *Construct a sand clock.*

To prove your hypothesis, pour the sand back into the two-liter bottle (use a funnel and be sure to get all possible particles back in). Time another run. Record the exact time (in minutes and seconds) in a log. Repeat the procedure, doing 10 runs. Each run must be within plus or minus one second for each minute in the run. The average of the runs is not important. Each run must fall within the accuracy specified. Reach a conclusion about your hypothesis.

Note that humidity can be a factor. Keep the moisture content of the sand constant. You might want to have an adult bake the soil, then seal it to keep moisture out.

Going Further

1. Graph the times obtained on your 10 runs.

2. Draw a scale on the milk jug to mark minutes. How do you compensate for the uneven leveling of the sand as it drops (it makes a mound higher in the center than at the sides)?

3. Replace the milk container with another soda bottle and build a stand to hold them. Then they can be flipped like an egg timer. Make sure the opening is not more restricted in one direction.

PROJECT 3-5
Metric Clock

Overview

The Babylonians were among the first great astronomers. As early as 1800 B.C., the Babylonians logged star positions on clay tablets. They are also responsible for dividing a day into 24 hour periods, an hour into 60 minutes, and a minute into 60 seconds.

Base 10 is much easier to work with in many respects. Our money is founded on the base 10 number system. Officials in our country are trying to slowly switch some measurements that are in "hard-to-work-with" forms—inches, feet, and yards—to metric measurements—centimeters, decimeters, and meters, which use base 10.

Hypothesize that you could make working with time easier by dividing a day into base 10 increments.

Materials

- old analog clock (with hands, not a digital clock)
- white construction paper
- marker
- protractor
- paste

Procedure

Paste a piece of white construction paper over the face of an old analog clock. Cut around the hands so that the hands will still be seen. Using a protractor, mark 10 even increments on the clock face. These will correspond to "decihours," or any other name you assign. There will be 36 degrees between each increment. Identify the marks with the numbers 1 through 10, where the number 5 is where a 6 is on a traditional clock, and a 10 will be at the top. Create "centihours" by marking 10 increments between each number on the clock face. There will be 100 of these marks on the clock face.

Going Further

Can you create a big enough clock face to break the increments down to "millihours"?

PROJECT 3-6
Booking Your Flight

Overview

As the Earth orbits around the Sun, the length of daylight changes. This is caused by the Earth's tilt on its axis, when the Northern Hemisphere faces the Sun during the summer and away from it during the winter. It is well known that some species of birds fly south for the winter. While it is not fully understood what "tells" the birds to begin their travel, much evidence points to the length of the day as being a trigger. The term "length of day" is used to mean the period of time the Sun is above the horizon on a given day (between sunrise and sunset). The shortest day (day of least sunlight) is December 21 or 22, depending on the year. The longest is on June 21 or 22.

Hypothesize that the trigger that starts bird's migration appears to be the length of day rather than other factors.

Materials

- research materials

Procedure

Gather research material on migrating bird species. Some migrating birds to study include robins, bluebirds, red-winged blackbirds, and most ducks and geese. Pay particular attention to the day each species begins to head south. If the month and day are the same every year (within a few days), this is strong evidence that the length of day is the cause. Study the swallows that leave mission San Juan Capistrano in California every year on, or about, October 23.

Be sure to show how other factors are not possible causes. For example, compare the temperature and weather conditions at each year on the day of their departure. Show how food cannot be a factor because the birds leave before the winter weather affects their food supply.

Going Further

How does the length of day affect other things? Consider animal mating behavior. How about crop planting? In the Land of the Midnight Sun, the northern part of Norway extending 300 miles into the Arctic Circle, two growing seasons can occur while only one takes place on the North American continent.

4

The

Solar System

Our closest astronomical neighbors are the Moon, the Sun, the planets, and an occasional comet. Because these objects are relatively close when compared to other objects in the sky, we can study and learn more about them. We have landed on the Moon. We have sent satellites to explore the planets and the Sun.

This chapter deals with the Moon, the Moon's effect on the Earth, eclipses, comets, and our solar system's planets.

PROJECT 4-1
Ebb and Flow
Adult Supervision Required

Overview

The Moon orbits around the Earth once every 29$\frac{1}{2}$ days but it is not always the same distance from the Earth. The Moon's orbit follows an elliptical (an oval-shaped) path. The effect of the Moon's gravitational force changes through the month as its relative position to the Earth changes.

Hypothesize that the gravitational pull of the Moon affects the tides on Earth. This hypothesis will be tested by measuring the high tide height during all phases of the Moon's monthly cycle. During the time of a full Moon, the height of the water level at high tide will be higher than at high tides during other lunar phases.

Materials

- access to a tidal body of water (preferably an ocean)
- tide chart for your area
- bulkhead
- long, 2-×-4"-piece of lumber
- 2 × 1" piece of lumber
- meter stick or yardstick
- logbook
- hammer
- nails
- paint and thin paint brush

Procedure

Using a yardstick or tape measure, paint inch marks (or other increments) along the 2-by-1-inch piece of lumber. Locate a tidal body of water. Have an adult drive the nail through the 2-by-4-inch piece of lumber and into a bulkhead to be used as a tide height reference point. It is most important that it be secure and not move for a month. At high tide, drive a small nail half way into the 2-by-1. Position it at the normal high tide mark.

Draw columns in a logbook to record the date, the phase of the Moon, and the height of the water at the time of high tide. The nail will be your reference point for determining a height value for high tide. Consider the nail to be the starting point, zero. If the water line at high tide is 1 inch below it, then record "1 inch below" in your logbook under the column heading "Height at high tide."

Each day at high tide, determine the water height in relation to the nail reference point. This might be a little difficult on stormy days if the water is rough. On rough days when the water has waves, watch the nail area for a little while and try to find the low point of the wave troughs and the high point of the wave crests. You might even want to make a baffle to hold in front of it to break waves while taking your reading. The point midway between the trough and the crest can be assumed to be the average height. Measure the distance from this midpoint to the reference nail.

Get a book that shows the various phases of the Moon. For one lunar month (29 days), keep a log indicating the date, the phase of the Moon, and the height of the tide (relative to the nail). After recording your data for a month, study your figures and reach a conclusion about your hypothesis.

Going Further

Which of a day's two high tides is higher? Is this true each and every day? How does the phase of the Moon play a part on tide height?

PROJECT 4-2
Shadow Boxing
Adult Supervision Required

STOP

Overview

You are, of course, familiar with your shadow, which you see anytime it is a bright day. Because the Sun shines constantly on the Earth, a shadow of the Earth extends out into space. Because the Sun is very wide, this source of light causes the Earth's shadow to have two parts. One part is an area of total shadow and is called the *umbra*. The second is a partial shadow, or *penumbra*. The umbra extends out into space about 857,000 miles, eventually coming to a point, making a cone shape. The penumbra is just the opposite. This shadowy area widens as the distance from the Earth increases. These shadows are shown in Fig. 4-1.

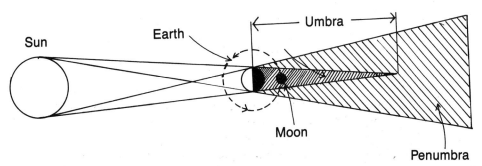

Fig. 4-1. *The Earth casts shadows into space, the umbra or total shadow area, and the penumbra, or partially shaded arcs.*

Outdoors on a sunny day, hold a pencil 1 inch above the ground. You will see the shadow of the pencil. Slowly move the pencil higher, away from the surface of the Earth. Notice that the shadow is being washed out as sunlight gets around the pencil and causes the shadow area to become more lighted.

A lunar eclipse occurs when the Moon's orbit causes it to pass into the Earth's shadow. At times, we only get a partial eclipse. Hypothesize that, as the umbra increases, so does the penumbra.

Materials

- solid rubber ball, about the size of a ping pong ball
- stiff cardboard, about 8½ x 11″

- piece of 2-×-8-×-4″ board
- piece of 2-×-2-×-4″ board
- 4 thumbtacks
- 2 D-cell batteries
- 2 flashlight bulbs (such as Radio Shack #272-1120)
- electric hookup wire (such as Radio Shack #278-1291)
- modeling clay
- ruler
- soldering pencil and solder **(caution: solder guns get very hot)**

Procedure

Have an adult solder 2- or 3-feet-long lengths of hookup wire to two flashlight bulbs. Solder the other ends to two D-cell batteries, which have been soldered in series. If you have a D-cell battery holder that holds two cells, it is better to use the holder instead of soldering the wires directly to the batteries. Another option is to place an on/off switch in series with one of the battery wires so the lamps can be easily turned off when not in use.

Construct the device seen in Fig. 4-2. As shown, lay an 8-inch-long piece of 2-by-4 board on a table. Use thumbtacks to secure a piece of cardboard to the board. On top of the board, rest a 2-inch-long piece of 2-by-4, stood up on end. Using modeling clay, place enough clay on top of the short 2-by-4 to be able to make a base that will keep a rubber ball from rolling off.

At about 7 or 8 inches from the surface of the ball, hold up one of the flashlight bulbs. It will cast a single dark shadow onto the cardboard. While continuing to hold the lit bulb, bring the second bulb very close to the first, almost touching it. Now the total light source is wider than it was with simply a single bulb. You will see light and dark shadow areas on the cardboard. These represent the Earth's umbra and penumbra shadows. Increase the distance between the light bulbs and the ball casting the shadow. Do both the umbra and penumbra increase?

Going Further

1. Change the distance between the shadow marker and the screen. Will the umbra and penumbra change in relationship?

2. Is there a relationship between the umbra and penumbra to the distance between the two bulbs?

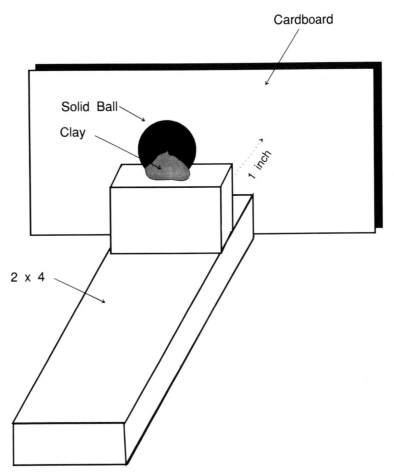

Cardboard

Solid Ball

Clay

1 inch

2 x 4

Fig. 4-2. *A device to examine umbra and penumbra areas.*

3. In the winter, the Earth is closer to the Sun. Does holding a book one foot above the ground in the summer cast a different shadow than holding the book one foot above the ground in the winter?

4. Using mathematics, can you calculate how far the Earth's shadow extends into space?

PROJECT 4-3
Traveling South
Adult Supervision Required

Overview

It is said that the Sun comes up in the east, but does it? Hypothesize that, because the Earth moves in more ways than just on its axis, the Sun will not come up exactly in the east every day all year long. This project will take several weeks in which to gather sufficient data.

Materials

- stiff cardboard, about $8^{1}/_{2} \times 11"$
- piece of 2-×-8-×-4" board
- popsicle stick
- 4 thumbtacks
- straight pin
- transparent tape
- compass
- modeling clay
- ruler
- fine-point marking pen
- tabletop by a window with either a clear view of the Sun at sunrise or of the Sun at sunset.
- utility knife

Procedure

Construct the device shown in Fig. 4-3. A clump of modeling clay is placed on the 2-by-4 about 1 inch from the end of the board. At the end of the board, use thumbtacks to secure a stiff piece of cardboard to the 2-by-1. Have an adult cut the rounded bottom off of a popsicle stick to make it have a straight edge. Using a piece of adhesive tape, secure a straight pin to the top of the popsicle stick. Push the straight-edge side of the stick into the modeling clay and secure it so it will stand on its own.

Place the device on a steady tabletop where it will have a clear view of the Sun at sunrise. If you do not have such a view, the project can also be done in a window where a sunset can be seen. In that case, change the project hypothesis to "the Sun doesn't always set exactly in the west." With a compass, align the board so that it faces exactly to the east (or west).

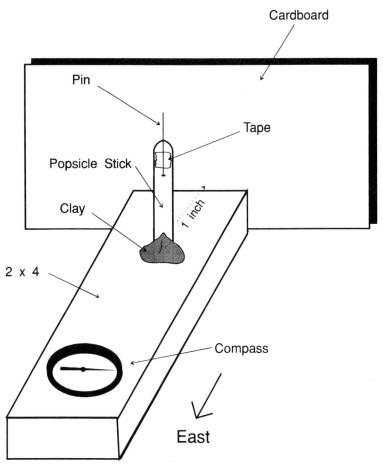

Fig. 4-3. *A device to investigate movement of the Sun.*

Each morning at sunrise (or each evening at sunset), carefully mark a thin line on the cardboard where the shadow of the straight pin falls on the cardboard "screen." Note the date. Do this each day or every other day. It might take several days before you notice any changes. Gather data for several weeks. There may be cloudy days when you will not be able to get a shadow. Nevertheless, if you gather data for a long time, a trend will be established.

Was your hypothesis correct?

Going Further

1. Consult with a pen pal at another latitude and longitude. Compare notes.

2. Follow the path of the Moon across the sky for an evening. Follow it for a year.

3. Can a Sun calendar for your latitude and longitude be constructed by marking the sunrise shadows for an entire year?

PROJECT 4-4
Comet Coming

Overview

A lot of astronomical work is done by evaluating photographs at great length. Such objects as comets can be discovered by examining two photographs of the same sky area and looking for any object that has changed position. In this project, you will use one of the modern day astronomer's tools, the computer. In a science fair, this project can be placed in either an astronomy or a computer category. Choose the category that has the fewest entries and you'll have less competition. Hypothesize that you can use a computer to simulate how astronomers compare photographs to find comets.

Materials

- personal computer that supports the BASIC programming language
- computer printer
- little knowledge of BASIC programming

Procedure

Using a computer, write a program that will randomly print asterisks on a sheet of paper and then print a second sheet with all the asterisks in the same positions except for one, which is to be slightly moved.

The program listed in Fig. 4-4 shows one example of how this might be done. This BASIC program was written on a PC-compatible computer. If you have a different computer, a few statements, such as those containing random number generation, might have a slightly different syntax. Refer to your computer owner's manual.

A traditional piece of typing paper contains 66 horizontal rows and 80 vertical columns when standard type (10 characters per inch) is used. The program sets up an array of 66 elements. A random number from 0 to 79 is stored in each array. One asterisk (*), representing a star or object in the sky, is printed on each of the 66 horizontal lines. The position on the line is determined by printing a random number of spaces, from 0 spaces to 79, then printing an asterisk. This allows the start to be placed anywhere from the first to the last printable column on the paper. The program shown uses the instruction to print a row of spaces:

```
LPRINT SPACE$(Y);
```

```
10 REM  Comet/photography simulation for "PC compatible" BASIC
20 DIM A(66) : REM  establish an array, 66 lines on a page
30 FOR X = 1 TO 66 : REM  do for each line on the page
40    Y = INT(RND * 80) : REM  pick a random # of spaces, 0 to 79
50    A(X) = Y : REM  store the random spacing number
60    LPRINT SPACE$(Y); : REM  print a row of random spaces
70    LPRINT "*" : REM  print an asterisk, representing a heavenly star
80 NEXT X
90 REM
100 Z = INT(RND * 66) + 1 : REM  randomly pick a line from 1 to 66
110 T = A(Z) : REM  store the current number of spaces on that line
120 A(Z) = INT(RND * 80) : REM  assign a new random # of spaces
130 IF A(Z) = T THEN GOTO 120 : REM  make sure the new number is different
140 REM
150 PRINT "Hit <ENTER> to print second page"
160 INPUT A$ : REM  wait for the user to position his paper
170 REM
180 FOR X = 1 TO 66 : REM  print another page, but with one * moved
190    LPRINT SPACE$(A(X));
200    LPRINT "*"
210 NEXT X
220 END
```

Fig. 4-4. *Computer program to simulate how astronomers compare pho-
tographic plates searching for comets.*

The number of spaces is determined by the value of variable Y.
If your computer's BASIC language does not support this instruction, you can replace it with a FOR/NEXT loop. For example:

```
FOR C = 1 TO Y
LPRINT " ";
NEXT C
```

After printing the first page, a second page is printed, with one
of the rows (picked randomly in program line number 100) having
its number of printed spaces altered. Line 100 stores the current
number of spaces and line 120 assigns a new value. Line 130
checks to make sure that the random number generator did not
happen to pick the same number again, otherwise the asterisk
would be printed in the identical spot.

Place both printed pages next to each other. Can you or your
friends spot which object moved? Hold both pages up to the light or
against a bright, sunny window, aligning the stars to see if any have
moved. Was your hypothesis correct?

Going Further

1. Print a different color for the changed asterisk (if you have a
   color printer) to highlight it.

2. The computer simulation program only simulated a comet moving in a horizontal direction. Write a computer program that will randomly move the object in both the horizontal and vertical planes.

3. Instead of printing the star chart on paper, use a split screen and light pixels.

PROJECT 4-5
Moon Map

Overview

The same side of the Moon always faces the Earth, so we only see one side. You might want to research why this is so and do a project on it. Even though we see the same side, the Moon changes position slightly, letting us see a little more than half of the Moon's surface during the month. This tilting motion lets us see about 59 percent of the Moon's surface. Hypothesize that the position of the side that faces us changes.

To prove your hypothesis, map the Moon's surface features each night for a month and compare any differences. Pay particular attention to the edges of the Moon.

Materials

- small telescope or pair of binoculars
- pencil and sketch pad
- dates for the phases of the Moon for the next month (often published in the newspaper)

Procedure

The Moon goes through a complete cycle of phases about every 29 days. Because part of the Moon is dark during this cycle, you will not be able to see the entire Moon's surface each day of the month. If you start sketching the features beginning with the first waxing crescent Moon, or more reflected light from the Moon, however, you can at least track those features throughout most of the Moon's phases.

Use a pair of binoculars or a small telescope to view any shapes and markings on the Moon that you see and draw them. Be very accurate. Record the phase of the Moon and the date on the drawing. Continue observing and sketching each night throughout the month (use a separate piece of paper for each sketch). At the end of the month, when the new Moon phase is reached and the Moon is no longer visible, compare each drawing. Did any of the Moon's features change position during the observed period? Is your hypothesis correct?

Going Further

1. Use a camera to take a photograph each night along with your sketches for additional comparison materials.

2. Do a project showing the Moon and Earth relationships that cause the Moon to reveal more than half its surface to us each month.

PROJECT 4-6
Look It Up

Overview

Comets are awe-inspiring sights to those who are fortunate enough to see the really spectacular ones. Over the years, much has been learned about these strange members of the solar system. Their long elliptical orbit takes many of them to the very edge of the solar system.

This project is not experimental in nature, and therefore, might not be suitable for upper-grade science fair students. It has merit, however, because of the interest many people have in comets and because it unites two science disciplines, astronomy and computers. Also, many comets are discovered by amateur astronomers. This project increases comet awareness.

Comets are a most unusual phenomenon and learning more about them and their characteristics helps us better understand our universe as a whole. This project involves setting up a database program on a computer to break down information about comets.

Materials

- personal computer
- database program
- research materials on comets (books, astronomy magazines, talk to professionals in the field)
- knowledge of computer use

Procedure

Set up a database program on a computer that will store information on comets. A commercially available database program can be used. Create fields for as many parameters as you can. Some suggestions include:
- Comet name.
- Discover's name (comets today are named both after their discoverer and the year they are discovered).
- Visible to the naked eye (yes/no).
- Date first seen.
- Date last seen.
- Date due to return.
- Comet family (Jupiter, Saturn, Uranus, Neptune group). Comets whose furthest traveling point from the Sun comes

close to a planet's orbit are considered members of a "comet family." There are about 30 known members of the Jupiter group, for example.
- Notable characteristics. Notable characteristics should include brilliance and the shape of the tail. Biela's comet split into two parts in 1846.
- Period (time it takes for one orbit around the Sun).

Talk to professionals in the field of astronomy to gather data. Research books and magazines for your database. Enable the database to be queried (asked questions of) by listing all the comets in the order in which they were discovered, sorted alphabetically by name, grouped by comet family, listed by date due to return, and by comparisons of notable characteristics.

Going Further

1. Instead of using a commercially purchased database program, write a comet database program using a computer language such as BASIC.

2. Create a database on other aspects of astronomy—the planets, stars, black holes, and quasars.

PROJECT 4-7
Far Away Sizes

Overview

Pictorial diagrams in books often depict the size relationships among the planets. They show Mercury as a tiny circle and Jupiter as a giant sphere. Other drawings represent the distance between planets. While these illustrations give the reader a feeling for the size and distance in comparisons to each other, they are not drawn to scale.

It is possible to create an accurate scale model of the planet sizes, however. Mercury, the smallest planet, has a diameter of 4,875 km. The largest planet, Jupiter, has a diameter of 142,700 km. You could establish a scale where 1 cm on the scale equals 1,000 km in real life. In this instance, Mercury would be about 5 cm in diameter (about 2 inches) and Jupiter 143 cm (about 56 inches or $4^{1/2}$ feet). That wouldn't fit on a page in a book but could be made into a tabletop exhibit. You would have to leave out the Sun, though, because it is so huge. Representing 1 cm to 1,000 km, the scale model would be about 14 meters (46 feet) in diameter!

It is also possible to create an accurate scale model showing the distance between the planets. Mercury, the closest to the Sun, is 58,000,000 km from it. Distance is measured by astronomers in *astronomical units*, or AU for short. One AU is the distance from the Earth to the Sun, 93 million miles. Mercury, then, is .39 AU. Pluto, usually the farthest planet, is 39.4 AUs. Setting a scale of, say 3 cm to 1 AU, all of the orbital distances could be represented in a little over a meter.

Although it is possible to represent planet sizes or planet distances to scale, it is not possible to have an exhibit that shows both size and distance to scale on the same model. Either some planets such as Mercury would be so small you would need a microscope to see them, or the distance to Pluto would be so far away that it might be in the next state.

Hypothesize that you can represent planet sizes or planet distances in accurate scale models but not both.

Materials

- balloons
- papier-maché
- small round objects such as ball bearings, marbles, golf

balls, baseballs, and similar spherical planet representatives
- research materials to find the diameter of each planet and their distance from the Sun
- calculator (optional)
- Christmas tree stand
- painter's aluminum extension pole with paint-roller handle on it
- Styrofoam balls
- knitting needle
- kite string
- glue
- measuring device (yardstick, meter stick)
- small piece of plywood
- eyehook with a screw base

Procedure

This exhibit will consist of two scale models. One will show the representative size of each planet to each other. Set them side by side on the table. Once you have established a scale, find or make round objects that match the correct size for each planet. Small planets can be represented by marbles, small stones and pebbles, and ball bearings. Medium-sized planets can be represented by balls used in various sports. Large planets might have to be constructed. Blow up large balloons and cover them with paper maché.

Another exhibit will show the distance between each planet. Use a painter's aluminum extension pole with a paint-roller handle on the end. Tie a string to the end of the paint roller. To get height, extend the pole as far as it will go and secure it by placing it in a Christmas tree stand. An alternative would be to use an orange or plastic milk crate, cutting holes in the sides through which the pole can be supported. Using a knitting needle, carefully poke a hole through the Styrofoam balls. The balls can all be the same size because their size cannot be accurately represented on this distance scale. Each ball represents a planet. Tie a knot in the string or use glue to fix each planet on the string at the correct distance from the Sun, with the top of the string being the Sun. Tie the bottom of the string to the tree stand or to a piece of plywood with an eyehook screwed into it (see Fig. 4-5).

Enhance your display with a chart that shows the scale sizes needed if it were possible to make a model representing both distances and planet sizes. Reach a conclusion about your hypothesis.

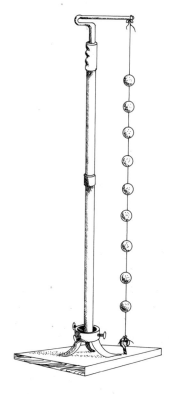

Fig. 4-5. *A model that shows the representation of distances.*

Going Further

1. Show the Sun's diameter using 3/8-inch washers to represent the Earth's diameter. Place the washers side by side across the Sun's diameter. How many washers will you need?

2. Calculate the volume. How many "Earths" could fit in a sphere the size of the Sun?

PROJECT 4-8
It Sure Looks Flat

Overview

Although it is not apparent when looking outside, the world is round. Early mankind thought it was flat and did not understand the things we do today. Nevertheless, hypothesize that you can offer simple proofs that the Earth is round.

Materials

- research materials
- access to a large body of water where ships travel
- collection of different shaped objects to cast shadows

Procedure

In this project, hypothesize that you can prove that the Earth is round. One proof that the Earth is round is to look at the Earth's shadow. During an eclipse of the Moon, the Earth's shadow is seen on the surface of the Moon. The shadow is curved. You can enhance your project by constructing a model that shows a sphere is the only shape that no matter what position it is in, it will always cast a circular shadow. Use a light and different shaped objects (flat, pyramid, conical, spherical) and project their shadows against a screen. You might include photographs of lunar eclipses in your project.

Another proof is to watch ships sailing out to sea. The ship will disappear from the bottom up until the mast is the last part visible. It could be argued that the ship sank or fell off the edge of the Earth, so a better proof would be to either speak to the shipmates upon their return or to watch a ship coming into port. You might want to even photograph a ship as it comes closer or sails further away to enhance your display at a science fair.

Can you think of any other proofs to prove your hypothesis?

Going Further

1. Collect photographs of the Earth taken from space by satellites and astronauts. These show the round Earth from afar.

2. Star constellations seen in the Northern Hemisphere are different from those seen in the Southern Hemisphere.

3. Identical objects weigh just about the same wherever they are on the Earth. Gravity pulls down equally in all directions toward the center of the Earth.

PROJECT 4-9
By the Light of the Silvery Moon

Overview

Planets are seen as reflected light. Reflecting is a function of the angle of incidence and the material it is made of. Reflection is the bouncing of light off of a surface. The angle made between the surface and the incoming light is the angle of incidence. You can measure the amount of light not absorbed because that which is not absorbed is reflected. Hypothesize that soil that has the least amount of reflectivity has the highest temperature because of absorption.

Materials

- 3 aluminum baking trays, about 8 × 10 × 1″
- 3 thermometers
- sunny window
- 3 types of soil, such as sand, sandy loam, and topsoil
- photographer's light meter

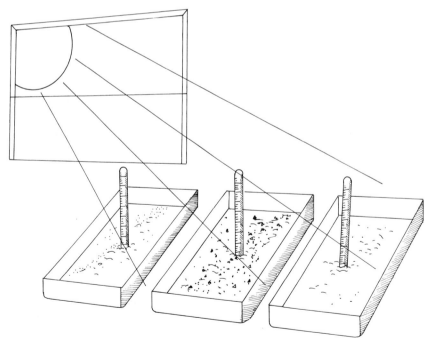

Fig. 4-6. *The soil on a planet with the least amount of reflectivity has the warmest temperature.*

Procedure

Fill three aluminum baking trays with three different types of soil. Insert a thermometer in each soil sample. Place the trays in a sunny window (see Fig. 4-6). Using a photographer's light meter, measure the reflectivity of each sample. After one hour, measure the temperature in each sample. Compare reflectivity with temperatures and reach a conclusion about your hypothesis.

Going Further

1. Experiment with soils or minerals of different color. Mars is a ruddy red, for example. Try orange gravel.

2. Some planets have a lot of rocks on their surfaces. Could you perform this experiment using rocks instead of soil?

3. How do smooth surfaces compare with uneven, rough surfaces?

PROJECT 4-10
The Blue Planet Effect

Overview

Some planets such as Mercury have virtually no atmosphere and some such as Venus have such a dense layer of clouds that the planet's surface cannot be seen. A planet's atmosphere is a big factor in controlling the planet's temperature. One atmospheric phenomenon that has made the news in recent years is what scientists call "the greenhouse effect."

The glass in a greenhouse lets sunlight through. The sunlight warms the objects inside the greenhouse but the glass prevents their radiated heat energy from escaping. So, the air inside the greenhouse warms up. Some scientists believe this is happening to the Earth. They believe that the buildup of gases, usually carbon dioxide, in the atmosphere forms a canopy or "greenhouse," preventing the gases close to the Earth from escaping as they normally should, creating higher global temperatures.

Many people are concerned about this phenomenon because rising Earth temperatures could melt the polar ice caps, raising the level of our oceans and possibly flooding low-lying coastal areas. It would also affect crop growth.

Hypothesize that the greenhouse effect produces more warming of a planet's surface than would be produced by the Sun's rays alone.

Materials

- 4 shoe boxes
- 4 thermometers
- adhesive tape
- table by a sunny window
- plastic food wrap
- scissors

Procedure

Remove the lids from four shoe boxes or other boxes of similar size and shape. Lay a thermometer on the bottom inside of each shoe box. Use adhesive tape to hold each thermometer in place. Using one or two shoe box lids, cut four squares, each about 2 inches square. Fold each in half making a triangular tent. Tape these tents over the bulb of each thermometer. These will act as covers to keep the bulb part of the thermometers out of direct sunlight.

The first shoe box will not have any covering on it. Place a single sheet of food wrap over the second box. Place two sheets of food wrap over the third box and three sheets over the fourth. Use adhesive tape to secure the sheets tightly to the top of the boxes.

Place all four boxes on a table in a sunny window (Fig. 4-7). After a half hour, read the temperatures on the four thermometers and record their readings. Did a greenhouse effect take place? Reach a conclusion about your hypothesis.

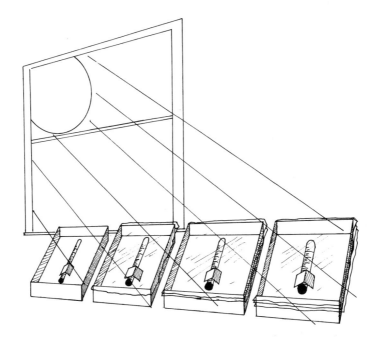

Fig. 4-7. *Testing for the greenhouse effect.*

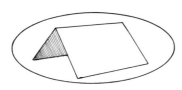

Going Further

1. Add a fifth box to the experiment, placing a 1/2-inch air gap between two layers of plastic food wrap. Does the addition of the insulated air gap increase the greenhouse effect?

2. Repeat the experiment but place the boxes out of direct sunlight. When only indirect light is available, does the greenhouse effect still take place?

3. The surface of planets differ in color. Paint the bottom of four shoe boxes white. Paint the bottom of four more black. Place thermometers in all eight and cover with different layers of plastic wrap (starting with no covering to a three-ply thick covering). Is there a relationship between the colored boxes and their coverings? For example, if the three-ply white box is twice as hot as the uncovered white box, is the three-ply black box also twice as hot as the uncovered black box?

4. Are scientists worried about something that nature can take care of itself? Is the greenhouse effect self-correcting? As the greenhouse effect causes temperatures to increase, the polar ice caps begin to melt. As they melt, they cause the oceans to spread out and cover more land area. This extra area of water reduces the amount of land that absorbs more heat from sunlight than the highly reflective water surface. The less land there is, the less surface area to absorb heat. Also, more water causes more evaporation, which causes more precipitation. Precipitation lowers temperature.

PROJECT 4-11
Where Is North?

Overview

If someone asks you to point exactly north, in which direction do you point? Would you use the North Star, or Polaris, as your reference? Would you pull out a compass and point in the direction the needle indicates? Would you look on a globe and point to the intersection of all the meridians (north- and south-running lines) on top of the Earth? Each of these directions are different!

Polaris is close to being in line with the north but it is not completely accurate. It is about one degree from the north celestial pole, an apparent axis around which the Earth rotates and points toward a place in the sky. The true North Pole, called the *terrestrial North Pole*, is the place where the meridians all meet at the top of a globe. The needle on a compass points to the Earth's "magnetic North Pole," which is deviated (strayed) from true north. "Magnetic deviation" is the number of degrees a compass needle will point away from the terrestrial North Pole. If the magnetic deviation in your area is determined to be 11 degrees west, that means the needle on a compass will point 11 degrees too far to the west. Therefore, true north is 11 degrees east of the compass reading.

Is the magnetic deviation decreasing, increasing, fluctuating, or staying the same over a century? Hypothesize that it is either increasing or decreasing steadily, but not fluctuating back and forth.

Materials

- research materials
- compass
- arts and crafts materials

Procedure

You will need to find the magnetic deviation in your area now and over the past century. Sources to check for this information include the library, a local airport, a weather station, the Coast Guard, and surveyors. Compile the data and reach a conclusion about your hypothesis.

Enhance your project's display by showing a compass pointing to the magnetic North Pole and, possibly, using string as vectors (lines with a direction), show the direction of the terrestrial North Pole from your area.

Going Further

1. What causes the deviation to change over time?

2. Can you think of locations on the Earth where you could point in the exact same direction for both the magnetic north and terrestrial north?

5

Beyond the Solar System

We cannot directly measure the stars and planets that we see in the night sky. We cannot touch them nor weigh them. Any information we learn must be gathered by detecting and measuring light and other forms of radiation they give off. Through the science of astronomy, mankind has gained much knowledge about heavenly bodies without traveling to them. Today, we are fortunate enough to have technology that is beginning to permit us to send probes to other planets to gather detailed information on a first-hand basis. Such gathering of information has never been possible at any other time in human history.

PROJECT 5-1
Pizza in the Sky

Overview

A "constellation" is a group of stars. These star clusters can be connected by imaginary lines to form shapes. Most everyone is familiar with the Big Dipper, seen in the constellation of Ursa Major. The grouping of constellations can be traced back as far as 3000 B.C. The early Egyptians, Greeks, and others used clusters of stars as points to form the shapes of people and animals. Characters in Greek mythology were given spots in the night sky, with certain arrangements of stars forming key parts of their outlines, such as the belt of Orion the hunter. In the absence of knowledge, imagination reigned, and many mythologies arose.

Hypothesize that you can create your own constellations based on modern objects. The early Greeks based their constellations on things that were familiar to them, such as animals, warriors, their imaginary gods. Base your constellations on objects that are familiar to people today.

Materials

- sketch pad and pencil
- clear evening outside
- tracing paper

Procedure

On a clear evening, choose an area of the sky and draw a detailed map of the stars that can be seen with the naked eye. Indoors, overlay a piece of tracing paper onto your sky map. Using the stars as key points, draw shapes of familiar objects. Think of as many modern-day objects as you can. Some suggestions; a floppy computer diskette, a soda bottle, a pizza. Make up a mythological story about the characters and objects you create. Do you see Mario running away from a field of mushrooms? Is your hypothesis correct?

Going Further

See if your objects are identifiable by your friends. If you tell them to look for these objects in the given area of the sky, can they imagine it too? Exchange ideas.

PROJECT 5-2
Circles of Light
Adult Supervision Required

Overview

The North Star, also called Polaris, appears to remain stationary, acting as a pointer toward the north on a compass. Mariners in the Northern Hemisphere have long depended on the North Star to assist them in navigating the oceans. This is because the stars in the sky move as the evening goes on but the North Star appears to remain in one spot. These stars trace the path of a circle during a 24-hour period. If you were to look at a part of those paths for just an hour or two, they would form the shape of an arc, a piece of a circle.

On a merry-go-round, the person who is on a horse closest to the center of the ride doesn't cover as much distance as a person on a horse on the outer edge, nor does the inner rider travel as fast. This can also be demonstrated using a record player turntable. Place a penny near the center spindle and a dime on the outer edge. Rotate the turntable a quarter of a turn. Which coin covered more distance? Which coin traveled faster?

Hypothesize that the stars closest to the North Star will have a path that seems longer than stars farther away. Note: These paths are due to the motion of the Earth, not of the stars.

Materials

- camera and film
- clear, Moonless night
- area away from light interference
- tripod to mount the camera
- star chart to locate the North Star
- push pin or straight pin
- 8½-x-11" sheet of thin cardboard
- pen
- ruler
- drawing compass

Procedure

Load your camera with the proper film for taking night pictures. This would probably be a "fast film" such as Tri-X. Your local camera shop employee should be able to give you good advice on the type of film for your camera. Mount the camera on a tripod. Locate the North Star in the night sky. Point the camera directly at it. Take three pictures, one hour apart. Don't move the camera between pictures.

When the pictures are developed, mark the top of each photograph. This will be a reference point to align the three photographs. Carefully, push a straight pin through the sheet of cardboard. Push the first photograph over the pin so that the pin sticks up through the North Star on the photograph.

Next, pick a bright star that is close to the center. Using a ruler, draw a line from the North Star through the inner bright star and extend it out off the photograph and onto the surrounding cardboard sheet. Similarly, pick a bright star that is farther away from the North Star. Draw a line from the North Star through the outer bright star and extend it out off the photograph and onto the surrounding cardboard sheet.

Next, push the second photograph, taken an hour later, over the pin, and align the top of the two photographs evenly. Identify the bright star that was close to the North Star. It should have changed position slightly. Draw a line from the North Star through the bright star and out onto the cardboard. You should now have a line on the cardboard indicating the first position and a line for the

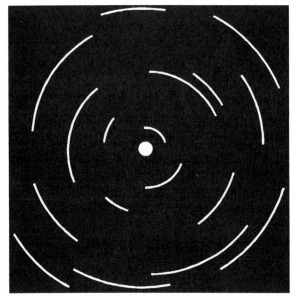

Fig. 5-1. *The light from stars traces area of a circle around Polaris using long-time exposures for photographs because of the movement of the Earth.*

second. Do the same with the outer star. Use a drawing compass. (How do you measure the length of the arc?)

Going Further

1. Map the stars you see near the North Star. What position does the Big Dipper have in relation to the North Star?

2. Try to use a video camera.

3. Use a camera that enables you to hold the shutter open for a long time. Mount the camera on a sturdy tripod. Aim the camera at the North Star. Leave the shutter open for an hour. Your photograph will trace the paths of stars forming an arc as they appear to rotate around the North Star in the center, as seen in Fig. 5-1.

PROJECT 5-3
What You See Is Not What You Get

Overview

As was discussed in Project 5-1, some stars seem to be gathered in groups. These groups are called constellations. Some familiar constellations include the Big Dipper and Orion The Hunter. Early man used stars as points making up the shape of a common object which they imagined to be in the sky, such as a bear or a hunter. Legends were made up about these figures.

Although these figures are valuable as reference points when identifying areas of the sky, they are only useful when viewed from Earth. At any other angle, they would lose their shape. To us, the stars appear to be in the same two-dimensional plane, but in reality, they exist in a three dimensional one. Hypothesize that the position of viewing a constellation is as significant as the objects themselves.

Materials

- black thread
- 4 cotton balls
- 8½-×-11″ sheet of thick cardboard
- string
- push pins
- adhesive tape
- optional: a few pieces of 1-×-2″ wood and nails to build an overhead support

Procedure

In this project, you'll construct a mobile and view it from all sides, including top and bottom, by hanging four cotton balls, each making up a corner of a square when viewed head-on. Because stars exist in a three-dimensional world, let the cotton balls hang in different planes. Use push pins or thumb tacks as tie points for the end pieces of black thread. Let each hang down to a position and length where they can be taped to the ends of the string to form a perfect square when viewed from the front.

It is best to hang the mobile from an overhead ceiling hook or lamp. This would allow unobstructed viewing from all sides except the top. If you put this project in a science fair where an overhead hook is not available, you might want to construct a support using a

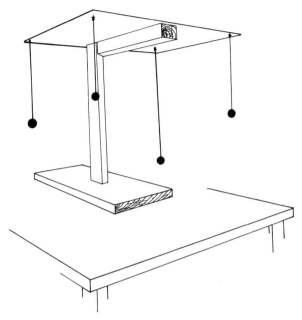

Fig. 5-2. *This mobile shows how the shapes of constellations would change if they were viewed from someplace other than Earth.*

few pieces of wood (have an adult assist in wood cutting and nailing). One suggestion is shown in Fig. 5-2.

Have volunteers stand several feet away and view your mobile. They should observe the four cotton balls as the four corners of a square. Ask them to move to different sides and have them describe the object they see.

This project should show that star patterns can be seen only from our own particular position in space. Reach a conclusion about your hypothesis.

Going Further

Can you make a geometric shape that looks like one object when viewed head-on but makes a completely different object when viewed on the side? Use a coat hanger to make your shape.

PROJECT 5-4
While Watching Their Flock

Overview

In our fast-paced modern world, people often tend to lose touch with nature. Even though our society has more time-saving conveniences, it is easy to become wrapped up in our day-to-day work and activities. When times were simpler, the average person was more aware of his environment. Think of the endless nights shepherds sat studying the night sky as they tended their sheep.

Hypothesize that the average person today will do poorly when asked simple astronomical questions. It is assumed that the common person in biblical times would have scored high on your questionnaire. It is assumed because we cannot go back in time and test shepherds.

Materials

- 20 or more adults who agree to take your quiz
- paper and pencils
- research materials
- optional: access to a copy machine
- optional: typewriter or computer with a word processing program and printer

Procedure

Make up a 10-question quiz with easy astronomy-related questions. These should be fairly simple and answerable with a YES/NO, TRUE/FALSE, or a short word. Do not use big, technical words or jargon. You are not trying to confuse anyone. Here are some ideas for your questions:

1. What was the phase of the Moon last night?

2. How many known planets are there in our solar system?

3. The side of the Moon where the lit, crescent part appears can indicate whether the Moon is in the first quarter of its phase or the last quarter. True or False?

While the questions should be easy and simple, do not make them all true and false. Even if a person did not speak English, there is a probability that he would get half of them right just by guessing.

Make 20 copies of your quiz and give them to volunteers. Be sure that the volunteers are adults and are not amateur astronomers, science teachers, or others involved in any job that would cause them to be especially knowledgeable about astronomy. Grade the tests and reach a conclusion about your hypothesis.

Going Further

Give the same quiz to eighth grade or high school students. Hypothesize that their test scores will average better than adult scores.

STOP

Project 5-5
Spread the Light
Adult Supervision Required

Overview

Why can't we study the stars in the daytime? Occasionally, we can see the Moon and even Venus during the day but light from the Sun washes out our view of the starlight. Even if we look in an area of the sky opposite the Sun, it is still too bright to see the stars. This is caused by diffusion (scattering) of the Sun's light as it hits particles in the atmosphere and is either reflected or absorbed.

Hypothesize that light is diffused in our atmosphere, reducing the ability to use optical astronomical equipment in daylight.

Materials

- candle and candle holder
- matches
- window facing a street or an area where the candle can be seen from far down the street
- yardstick

Procedure

Have an adult light a candle and safely place it in a window. The window must have a clear line of view far down the street or into any clear area. Measure your stride (the distance from one foot to the other as you walk). Walk far away from the candle in the window. When you get to the point where you can no longer see the light, record the distance, using paces.

Going Further

1. Try different nights under different conditions. Define the nights that astronomy works best—clear, overcast, hot, cold, or high or low humidity. When your candle can be seen at the greatest distance, these are the nights best for astronomy observation.

2. Can astronomy equipment that is not optical, such as infrared or radio astronomy, continue to be used during the day?

3. Walk as far as you can from the candle until it is just barely seen. Have a person shine a bright flashlight at you but not block your view of the candle. Does the bright light from the flashlight affect your ability to still see the candle?

PROJECT 5-6

Polaris Is Not a Submarine

Overview

If a stranger came to your town and asked you how to get to the local pharmacy, you might say "Drive down to the end of this street and make a left onto Elm Street. Go two more blocks, and turn right onto Main Street, go one block, and it will be on your left." You would use direction, street names, and measured lengths to identify where the pharmacy is located.

How does an astronomer locate objects in the sky and be able to tell another astronomer where to look? What does he use as universal reference points?

Hypothesize that you can identify a dozen stars around Polaris and reidentify them on another night. You can number them 1, 2, 3, an so on.

Materials

- materials or someone knowledgeable to show you which star in the evening sky is Polaris
- drawing compass
- poster board and pen or marker

Procedure

Locate Polaris, the North Star, in the evening sky. With the naked eye, find the star that appears to be closest to Polaris. Extend your arm and hold a drawing compass at arms length (Fig. 5-3). As you look at Polaris, place one tip of the compass on Polaris and the other on the closest star you can find. This gives you a relative distance between Polaris, a good universal reference point, and a star. Do not let the distance the drawing compass is spread apart change as you work with it.

Mark a spot in the center of the poster board and label it Polaris. Place the pointed end of your drawing compass on the Polaris mark. The pencil point end will rest on the page at the relative distance from Polaris as the star you observed outside. Mark East, West, North, and South on your poster board star map. Mark the spot where the closest star was seen that evening in the sky with respect to the four directions.

With a drawing compass, make a light circle that passes through your closest star point. Because the Earth is turning, the

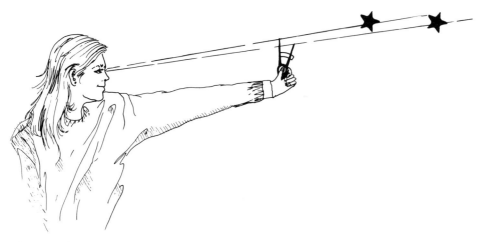

Fig. 5-3. *Find the relative distance between Polaris and other stars by using the point and pencil tip of a drawing compass held at arms length.*

star you observed tonight might appear in a different direction every night. But you can still identify your star, however, because all of the stars appear to rotate around Polaris and you now have a distance relationship—you know the star must fall somewhere on that circle. Add more stars using this method and map out an entire area of the sky.

Going Further

1. Are there other ways to identify a star's position? Consider the sky to be the inside of a bowl. Make East represent a 0 degree mark with counterclockwise (or clockwise) direction of increment up to 360 degrees. Take height into consideration, with the horizon representing 0 degrees and straight overhead 90 degrees.

2. Take four photographs of the area around Polaris. The photo of the sky section east of Polaris should show Polaris in the left side of the photo. The north photo should show Polaris in the bottom of the picture. Develop the pictures and overlap them, placing a pin through Polaris as the center.

3. Use other identifiable objects in the sky as reference points, such as the Big Dipper, the belt of Orion, or the Pleiades star cluster.

PROJECT 5-7
The Lactose Way

Overview

We live in the Milky Way Galaxy, a huge clustering of stars. We can see a band that is white in color stretch across the evening sky. We are looking edge-on at our galaxy. Hypothesize that there are more stars visible to the unaided eye in this white band than at other areas of the sky because of this clustering.

Materials

- empty paper towel roll
- pencil and paper
- magnetic compass

Procedure

We will use an empty cardboard paper towel roll to look through at different areas in the sky. Using a compass to locate direction, hold the paper towel roll in a dozen different directions (east, west, north, northeast, etc.) and at different elevations. Look in every area of the sky except where the white Milky Way Galaxy band is seen. Look through the roll and count the number of stars you see at each sample point. Record this number. When done, total up the number of stars seen and divide by the number of sample observations made. This will give you the average number of stars found in the area.

Locate the white Milky Way Galaxy band. Take several samples looking through the roll at different points. Total the number of stars seen and divide by the quantity of observations.

Was your hypothesis correct?

Going Further

Use a camera and a telescope to visually document your results.

6

Meteors and Meteorites

Have you ever looked up on a clear night and seen a streak of light flash across the sky? Meteors are quite common, and if you are patient, you can see one on just about any clear night. A meteor is a rocklike chunk of metal and stone that falls from space through the Earth's atmosphere. While no one is sure exactly where in space they come from, scientists generally believe most meteorites originate in the asteroid belt between Mars and Jupiter.

Some *meteor showers*, or groups of many meteors, can be seen on a regular basis. They are caused by large clumps of rocks that orbit the Sun. Every year, the path of the Earth's orbit crosses several groups of space debris, giving us a meteor shower display. During these times, as many as one meteor a minute can be seen. Figure 6-1 shows the approximate dates when these meteor showers occur each year. On these dates, you can lay outside and count the number of meteors without taking your eyes off the sky by using the traditional method of dropping beans in a bowl.

Meteors travel through the air at speeds of 20 to 45 miles per second (that's 162,000 miles per hour!). The heat from air friction makes them glowing hot, giving them the name *fireballs* or *shooting stars*. Even meteors that are only the size of a dime can generate enough light to be visible on Earth. Meteors stop burning about 5 to 20 miles above the ground.

When a meteor survives its travel through the atmosphere and impacts the Earth, it is called a *meteorite*. Meteorites are generally placed in one of three major classifications: stony, iron, and stony-iron.

Stony meteorites are similar to rocks found on Earth, being made up mostly of silicates with metallic iron particles scattered throughout them. Most meteorites are of the stony type.

Iron meteorites are composed almost wholly of iron (typically 85 percent to 95 percent) with the rest being mostly nickel and a small amount of other trace elements. Iron meteorites total about 5 percent of all meteorites.

The last category is stony-iron. Only about 1.5 percent of all meteorites are of the stony-iron type. These meteorites are composed of iron filled with rock materials.

With all of these rocks falling from space, you might think it would be dangerous to live on Earth. While there are no confirmed records of anyone ever being killed by a meteorite, there have been close calls.

In 1908, a meteorite that some scientists think was one of the largest known to hit the Earth in modern times, impacted in Siberia, killing 1,500 reindeer (some scientists believe it was a "black hole"). It is reported that a man who witnessed the event from 50 miles away was knocked unconscious. Before he passed out, he felt so hot that he thought his clothes where going to catch fire!

In 1847 in Bohemia, three children lay sleeping in a house where a 40-pound meteorite crashed into their room but did not harm them. In Illinois, a meteorite roared through a garage roof and into an automobile while the owner stood only 50 feet away. One woman lay sleeping on her living room couch when a meteorite crashed through the roof and hit her in the hip, bruising her.

Interestingly, one person's life was reportedly saved by a meteor shower! A man who would normally have been asleep in bed was outside viewing the Persieds meteor shower when his house caught fire and burned to the ground.

In this chapter, projects deal with such topics as identifying meteorites, determining where and how much meteorite material is located around an impact crater, and comparing the relative age of craters.

Meteorites let us touch a piece of space. Not only are they thrilling to hold, imagining what sights in the universe they have seen, but they are important to scientists who study space by helping them better understand our wondrous universe.

PROJECT 6-1
The Sky Is Falling

Overview

If you have ever skimmed a rock across a lake or discarded an unwanted rock from your garden, you may have let a meteorite slip through your fingers. Even though meteorites are more abundant than most people realize (about 3,500 fall to Earth each year), the average person does not recognize a meteorite when it is seen in nature. There are many reported cases where people did not know they had a meteorite and used it as a stone when building walls, as an anchor weight in fence buildings, even as a doorstop and paperweights. This project can help promote meteorite awareness and perhaps enable you to make a meteorite find one day.

Hypothesize that you can perform a series of tests to determine whether a rock is a terrestrial rock (one normally found on Earth) or a meteorite from outer space.

Materials

- collection of rocks from your area, from friends, or gathered while traveling on vacation
- magnet
- thread
- hand lens (magnifying glass)
- small scale (a postal scale or kitchen weight-watchers scale)
- hammer
- chisel
- rotating corundum or emery wheel
- paper and pencil
- bowl
- beaker large enough to hold the biggest rock sample
- small cup or other container

Procedure

If there is a museum or university near you that has meteorites, study their collection before beginning your project so you will know what they look like. If you pick up a rock that looks out of place, whose appearance is unlike other rocks in the area, you should examine it very closely.

Develop a chart such as the one shown in Fig. 6-2 to help study the properties of your sample rocks to see if they might be meteor-

Shower Name	Approximate Date Of Peak
Quadrantids	Jan 3
Lyrids	April 20 - 22
ETA Aquarids	May 4
Persieds	Aug 11 - 12
Orionids	Oct 21
Leonids	Nov 17
Geminids	Dec 13

Fig. 6-1. *Approximate dates of annual meteor showers.*

Identifying Rock Sample Number:		
Properties	Meets These Qualifications	Doesn't Meet Qualifications
Appearance		
Texture		
Composition: iron presence		
Density		

Fig. 6-2. *Chart to help study properties of rock samples.*

ites. One chart will be needed for each rock sample you test. As you perform each test, place your results on the chart. The following are some of the characteristics you will check:

- *Appearance.* The first property to check is appearance. Iron meteorites have irregular shapes, being angular. Check for a thin dark crust. This "fusion crust" was formed when the surface of the meteorite started melting from friction as it entered the atmosphere. Examine color. If the meteorite fell recently, it will be black or dark colored. If it is old, the iron will have begun to rust, making it more brown or yellowish brown in color. Soil also forms brown stains on meteorites that have been on the ground for a long time. Meteorites come in all sizes and shapes but are seldom symmetrically round.

- *Texture.* Meteorites are solid and not porous. Edges are smooth, dull, and gently curved rather than sharp. The surface might have pits that resemble oval thumb prints. There might be tiny bubbles on the surface caused by the surface melting in its last moments of flight.

- *Composition.* Most meteorites contain a large amount of iron. Tie a piece of thread to a small magnet and suspend it next to the sample rock. Gently swing the magnet toward the rock and feel if there is any attraction. If the magnet is attracted to the rock, then iron is present.

  Hold the sample rock briefly against a rotating corundum or emery grinding wheel. Using a hand lens, look for shiny, glittering specks of metal.

- *Density.* Because most meteorites contain a lot of iron, they are usually heavier than Earth rocks of the same size. They are solid throughout. Scientists have developed a number value called *specific gravity*, which they use to determine the relative density of all rocks and minerals that are heavier than water. Specific gravity is the relationship between the weight of a rock and the weight of the water it displaces.

To measure specific gravity, weigh the sample rock on a scale. Record its weight. Weigh a small, empty cup or other small container and record its weight. Fill a beaker to overflowing with water. When the overflowing water has stopped, position the small cup under the beaker's spout. Tie a piece of thread to the rock sample and gently lower it into the beaker until the entire rock is sub-

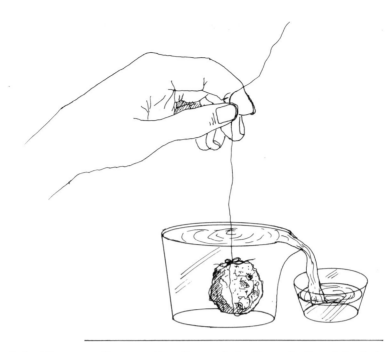

Fig. 6-3. *The specific gravity of a rock is the relationship between the weight of the rock and the weight of the water it displaces.*

merged under water (Fig. 6-3). The cup will collect the overflowing water the rock displaces.

When the flowing stops, weigh the cup that contains the displaced water. Subtract the weight of the cup from the total weight of the cup and water. This will give the weight of the displaced water. Divide the weight of the displaced water into the weight of the rock. The resulting figure is the specific gravity.

Determine the specific gravity of each rock you have collected. Most meteorites have a specific gravity of 3.3 or more, while most Earth rocks are less than 3.3.

After completing all tests, examine the data you have collected on the charts. If you find a rock specimen that passes your tests and you think may be a genuine meteorite, you might want to send it to a laboratory for further analysis. Addresses for these laboratories are given in the Appendix.

Going Further

Organize a meteorite hunt. Professional meteorite hunters often recommend looking in piles of rocks that farmers have gathered and removed from their fields (be sure to get permission to be on other people's property). Because Kansas, Texas, and New Mexico have very few rocks, meteorites there are easier to spot, resulting in these states having high meteorite finds. Research past newspapers to see where meteors or fireballs have been sighted. Subscribe to newsletters that report recent fireball sightings such as *Meteor News* and the Smithsonian Institute's *Scientific Event Alert Network* reports (see Appendix for addresses).

Catch a Falling Star

Overview

Evidence of past meteorites are scarce because the Earth is a dynamic system, with the natural forces on Earth such as wind, rain, vegetation growth, and earthquakes constantly altering its surface. Nevertheless, some meteor craters still remain visible today. The most famous one in the United States is Meteor Crater in Arizona. Thousands of pieces of meteorite have been recovered from the area surrounding the crater. Scientists estimate that a chunk of iron measuring about 25 meters across and weighing more than 10 million tons was responsible for forming the crater. The actual meteorite has not been found in one big piece.

How might scientists accurately guess the total mass of a meteorite that formed a crater? One way is by "sampling." The sampling technique evaluates the number of items in a particular area and from that representative sample comes up with an intelligent estimate as to the number of items in the whole area.

Hypothesize that by using the sampling method—measuring the pieces found in a representative area—you can determine the size of a fallen meteorite.

Materials

- small marbles
- yardstick
- protractor
- string
- small stepladder
- flat, level ground area
- masking tape and pen

Procedure

Count the number of marbles you have and record this number. Locate a relatively flat, level area on the ground, perhaps on a large patio, driveway (unpitched), or an unobstructed floor area in a big room. Using two strips of masking tape, mark an X on the floor. This will be considered the center of impact.

Standing on a small stepladder, drop all of the marbles at once onto the X. They will scatter. When all the marbles have come to a resting position, carefully remove the ladder. Tape one end of a piece of string on the *X* and extend it out from the center in a straight line beyond the point where the furthest marble rests. Cut the string and tape this end down. Tape another piece of string on the *X* and pull it out in a straight line as you did the last piece but at an angle of 10 degrees from the other line. Use the protractor to measure the angle.

Count the number of marbles that fell within the 10-degree-area slice. Record this sample number. Multiply the sample number by 36, because there are 360 degrees in a circle. This number is your estimate of the total number of marbles that fell. How does this number compare to the actual number that were dropped? Was your hypothesis correct?

Going Further

Hypothesize the size of a meteor by determining how big the hole is and how far the ejecta (material) is thrown. Use marbles and steel shot on sand.

PROJECT 6-3
Sliding into Home Plate

Overview

The last project, "Catch a Falling Star," hypothesized that the total size of a meteorite can be determined even if the meteorite has broken into many pieces. This was done by evaluating the number of pieces found in a representative area around the impact. The pieces in a 10-degree-angle slice of a circle were counted. Because there are 360 degrees in a circle, you can multiply the representative number of pieces found in a 10-degree slice by 36 to determine the mass of the whole. But that project assumed meteorites hit the Earth by coming straight down and its broken pieces scattered more or less equally in all directions. What if it hit the Earth at an angle? How would that affect the dispersion of meteoric material?

Many meteors blow apart when entering the atmosphere, and it is probably accurate to say that the one that caused the great Meteor Crater in Canyon Diablo, Arizona must have been one large mass. Yet, the bulk of this projectile has not been found. Diggings in the crater floor have not yielded this mass. It was thought that the meteor may have traveled from the north, lodging the projectile underneath the southern rim of the crater. Shafts drilled in this area flooded at a depth of about 200 meters, however, and it has been too expensive for further investigation to take place.

Hypothesize that meteorites that impact at an angle cause a greater percentage of meteoric material to be concentrated beyond the strike point than behind it (east or west, for example).

Materials

- small marbles
- large balloon
- yardstick
- water
- flat, level ground area outside
- masking tape

Procedure

Count the number of marbles you have and record this number. Fill the balloon with the marbles and water. Locate a relatively flat, level area on the ground, perhaps on a large patio, driveway (unpitched), or an unobstructed floor area in a big room. Using two strips of masking tape, mark off a quadrant, making a + as shown in Fig. 6-4. The middle point where the two tapes intersect will be considered the center of impact. Mark the directions (east, west, north, and south) and number the quadrants 1 through 4.

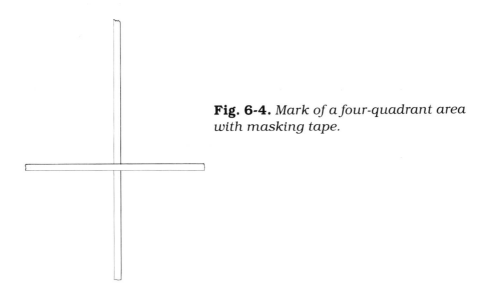

Fig. 6-4. *Mark of a four-quadrant area with masking tape.*

Stand back a few feet from the taped area and toss the water balloon at an angle so that it lands on the center mark. When the balloon breaks, the marbles will scatter. When all the marbles have all come to a resting position, count the number of marbles in each quadrant. Compare the quantity found in each quadrant with the total number of marbles you started with. To find the percentage of each quadrant, divide the total marble count (the "whole") by the number found in the quadrant (the "part") and multiply the answer by 100.

$$\frac{\text{part}}{\text{whole}} \times 100 = \text{percent}$$

Was your hypothesis correct?

Going Further

Instead of a water balloon, use a chute to drop the marbles at the impact point for angle and speed control.

PROJECT 6-4
On the Straight and Narrow

Overview

Meteors travel at speeds of 45 miles per second in space. When they enter the Earth's atmosphere, the air offers resistance, slowing them down. If a meteor is coming in at an angle, does the slowing down from this air resistance allow gravity to have more time to exert a pull on the meteor, changing its angle to be more perpendicular to the Earth's surface? Do denser meteors align to be perpendicular quicker than less dense ones?

Hypothesize that the more dense an object, the quicker it will change angles to become perpendicular with the Earth's surface because it is traveling through a medium.

Materials

- marble
- golf ball
- steel ball bearing
- small scale (a postal or food scale)
- water
- beaker large enough to hold a golf ball
- small cup
- fish aquarium
- masking tape
- 2-foot-length of corner molding
- pen or marker
- drawing protractor
- ruler

Procedure

Physicists have developed a ratio called *specific gravity*. Specific gravity compares the density of any substance to the density of some other substance. Scientists use specific gravity to determine the relative density of rocks and minerals by weighing the rock and the water it displaces. In this experiment, you will need to measure the specific gravity of each sample object—the marble, golf ball, and steel ball bearing.

To measure specific gravity, weigh the sample on a scale, and record its weight. Weigh a small empty cup or other small container and record its weight. Fill a beaker to overflowing with water. When the overflowing water has stopped, position the small cup under the beaker's spout. Gently lower the sample into the beaker until it is completely submerged underwater. The cup will collect the overflowing water that the sample displaces.

Once the flowing stops, weigh the cup that now contains the displaced water. Subtract the weight of the cup from the total weight of the cup and water. This will give the weight of the displaced water. Divide the weight of the displaced water into the weight of the sample. This result is the figure for specific gravity.

Next, fill an aquarium tank with water. Place a strip of masking tape lengthwise on one side near the bottom as shown in Fig. 6-5. Similarly, run a strip of masking tape along the same side lengthwise across the top. Using a ruler, mark a point on each strip to indicate the center point (from left to right). This will establish a base point where the rolling sample object will enter the water.

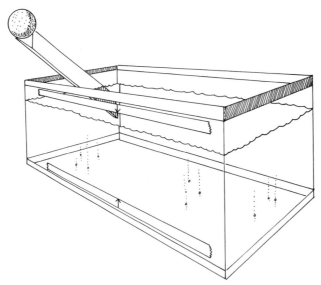

Fig. 6-5. *When an object travels through a medium such as air or water, friction and gravity can affect the object's path.*

Using a protractor, hold a 2-foot piece of corner molding at a 45-degree angle to the water level. Position it so that it makes a *V* chute for the objects to roll down. One end of the molding should just touch the water in line with the entry base point marked on the tape. Roll a marble down the chute. Start it at the end of the chute, letting it go so it can begin rolling. Do not push it.

On the masking tape, mark the point where it lands on the bottom. Measure the distance from the base point to the landing point. Record this distance on the chart. Repeat this procedure for the golf ball and ball bearing. Compare the distances and densities on the chart. Reach a conclusion about your hypothesis.

Going Further

Calculate the slope and slope angle with the track and a marble.

PROJECT 6-5
Old as the Hills

Overview

While the dynamic forces of erosion and constant change on Earth have erased evidence of most meteorite craters on Earth, the Moon, Mars, and other heavenly bodies that lack an atmosphere are covered with craters. On these bodies, we can often find places where two craters overlap. Although we can't easily travel to these places, hypothesize that we can determine which crater was created first at locations where the rim of one crater intersects another. The newest crater in an overlapping pair will have a complete circular rim, but the one that was there previously, will have its rim interrupted where the newer crater intersects it (Fig. 6-6).

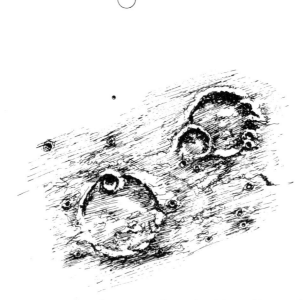

Fig. 6-6. *Where two craters have overlapping rims, the crater whose rim is perfectly intact is not as old as the other.*

Materials

- old, throwaway cake pan or disposable aluminum baking tray
- about 12 pounds of wallboard joint compound (available at hardware stores)

- smooth, round-shaped rock or stone, about 3 or 4″ in diameter
- water
- large spoon

Procedure

A medium is needed that is flexible enough to move, yet strong enough to retain it shape when a rock impacts it. The consistency of the material must be able to retain the shape of a slightly elevated crater lip when struck with a rock. It might be a good idea to experiment with different media, such as flour and water or plaster of paris. We found wallboard joint compound to work well.

Fill the old cake pan (one that can be thrown away) or the disposable aluminum baking tray with wallboard joint compound. Mix it thoroughly.

Thoroughly wet a smooth rock. Drop it from a height of about 4 feet above the surface so that it will create an impact "crater" in the mix. Carefully lift the rock straight up to remove it. Rinse it clean with water. Again, drop the rock into the mix, but this time drop it 2 inches off the center of the first crater so that the second crater rim overlaps the first. If your aim is off, simply smooth out the mix and repeat the procedure. Let the mix dry several days.

Is the second crater completely round and the first one distorted? Was your hypothesis correct?

Going Further

1. Enhance your display by painting the craters to resemble a scene on the Moon.

2. Wallboard compound forms cracks as it dries, resembling earthquake faults. If any of these cracks pass through your crater rims, can you hypothesize which geologic event occurred first, the meteorite impact or the earthquake?

3. Does the splash angle tell which direction a meteorite came from?

PROJECT 6-6
Surfing Mars

Overview

The surface of Mars shows evidence that water played a part in its geologic history. Yet today, it appears to be a desert. Planetary scientists believe that water is still present in the form of water-soaked soil that has frozen. In the future, scientists will send more unmanned robot spacecraft to Mars to further test the ground.

Can we speculate where ice deposits might be hidden on Mars by examining the characteristics of meteor craters? In this project, you will drop a rock into dry sand, wet sand, and frozen, water-soaked sand to determine if there is a difference in appearance in the craters produced. If there is, then perhaps scientists could study photographs of Mars to try to locate frozen water under the planet's surface. Hypothesize whether or not you think there will be significant differences in the appearance of the craters produced.

Materials

- 3 large, flat bedpans or trays, about 2 or 3″ deep and at least 8 × 8″
- water
- sand
- large stone or rock
- mixing spoon
- use of a freezer

Procedure

Fill the three large trays with sand. Add water to two of the pans and mix thoroughly until the sand is saturated with water. Place one of the water-soaked trays in a freezer.

After several hours, remove the frozen sample in the freezer. From a height of about 5 feet, drop a heavy stone or rock into each sand sample (Fig. 6-7). Examine the craters made in each case. Look for different characteristics in the shape of the craters, the amount of ejecta (material thrown out of the crater) surrounding the craters, the depth of the craters, and the height of the crater walls.

Was your hypothesis correct? Can you identify experimental crater characteristics to those on Mars? How about the Moon?

Fig. 6-7. *Drop a rock into different solid samples and examine the crater's shapes and ejecta amounts.*

Going Further

1. Examine pictures of Mars taken by the Viking spacecrafts. Do craters at the poles look different than craters at the equator?

2. Instead of dropping a rock (which simulates a meteorite hit), use a fan (which simulates wind) to blow air across each sample.

3. How much water can be contained in a given amount of soil? This might help determine if a small or large amount of water can be trapped in Martian soil.

PROJECT 6-7

The Height of Old Smokey

Overview

Unmanned spacecrafts have taken extraordinary photographs of the Moon, Mars, and other planetary bodies in our solar system. Although these photos are two dimensional, showing only the length and width of an area, scientists can determine the depth of craters and the height of mountains and rock formations. The photographs accurately measure the length and width of the surface area. Scientists also know the angle of the Sun to the planet's surface at the time the photographs were taken.

This project demonstrates how scientists can create a three-dimensional model of a planet's surface by knowing the angle of the Sun and the scale (length and width in accurate measurements) of the area from a two-dimensional photograph.

Materials

- desk lamp
- large protractor
- string
- ruler
- adhesive or masking tape
- flat tabletop
- large stone or rock (more than 3″ tall)
- graph paper
- pencil

Procedure

Tape a sheet of graph paper to a flat tabletop. Place a large rock on the paper at one end. A foot or more from the rock, position a desk lamp and point it toward the rock. Using the grid on the graph paper and a ruler, measure the length of the shadow cast by the rock. With a protractor, measure the angle of the light as shown in Fig. 6-8. This can be done by taping one end of a piece of string to the paper where the tip of the shadow falls and pulling the string tight to the center of the desk lamp's bulb. Stand the protractor upright using the table surface as a baseline and the string will mark the angle.

On a separate piece of graph paper, measure and mark off units on both an X (horizontal) and Y (vertical) axis. Knowing the angle of

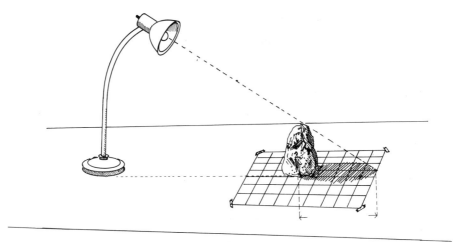

Fig. 6-8. *By knowing the angle of the Sun and the length of the shadow cast, the height of a mountain can be determined from a two-dimensional photograph of a planet's surface.*

the light source and the length of the shadow, draw the shadow length along the X axis. Draw a straight line beginning at the end of the shadow mark to the Y axis at the angle of the light source (Fig. 6-9). The height measured on the Y axis represents the height of the rock.

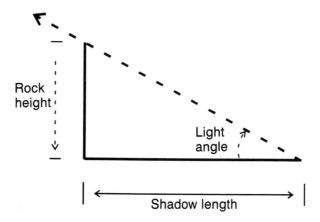

Fig. 6-9. *By knowing the angle and the length of the shadow cast, the rock height can be determined.*

Going Further

Math students can use geometry and trigonometry to calculate the rock height. What is significant about a shadow when the angle of the Sun is 45 degrees? (Hint: an isosceles triangle)

PROJECT 6-8

Persieds Showers
Bring August Flowers

Overview

Have you ever gazed into the night sky and seen a momentary streak of light? It is not uncommon to see a "shooting star," whose fast moving white trail can be seen for one to three seconds. When swiftly moving particles strike the Earth's atmosphere, friction causes them to heat up and burn. Most of these "meteors" vaporize and never reach the ground. While it is possible to see a shooting star on any clear evening, it is known that on certain nights of the year, an increasing number can be seen, causing what is known as a *meteor shower*.

Because these meteor showers appear to come mainly out of one area of the sky, these annual showers are given the name of the constellation from which they seem to originate. Meteors from Leo are called Leonids and meteors from Perseus are called Persieds, for example. The name of the annual meteor showers and the approximate date when their activity peaks were shown previously in Fig. 6-1 (Project 6-1 "The Sky Is Falling").

In some years, these showers are disappointing, with only a few meteors being seen. Other years produce as many as one meteor a minute, however. The best known shower was the Leonids in 1799. Thousands of meteors per hour were seen, looking like snow falling in the sky. Hypothesize that there is a pattern for each annual meteor shower regarding "good" (many meteors) years and "bad" (few meteors) years.

Materials

- research materials
- logbook

Procedure

Using library books and researching old magazines on astronomy, find out which years had high meteor activity for each of the annual meteor showers mentioned in the Overview. Make a logbook with the horizontal rows for the year (like 1991, 1990, 1989) and label it starting with the current year and going back as far as you

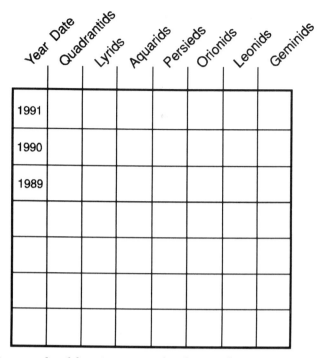

Fig. 6-10. *Research old astronomy books and magazines and see if some annual meteor showers exhibit more meteors per hour during some years than others.*

can get information on. Some astronomy books will tell you about high-activity showers in the past, such as the Leonids in 1799. Column headings will be the names of the showers (see Fig. 6-10). Write the number of meteors seen per minute in each entry on the chart. If you don't have that information, simply write "good" year or "bad" year, indicating that there was a peak of high activity or that it was no better than it is every year.

Your research will reveal any patterns (Note: Leonids peaks every 33 years). If patterns are discovered, then you will be able to predict when the next big showers will occur.

These meteor showers are caused by great rings of particles that have elongated elliptical orbits around the Sun (Fig. 6-11). When the Earth's orbit causes it to pass through the path of these particles, a meteor shower can be seen. If there is a clustered group of particles around the ring, there is a spectacular shower. It is this concentrated swarm you should be looking for in this project.

Reach a conclusion about your hypothesis.

Going Further

1. Use graph paper to chart the activity rates per year for each shower.

2. How far away do we see meteors? If you see a meteor in your town, will someone in the next town be able to see it? In the next state? In the next country?

7

Other Uses for the Stars

The sky has always been mysterious; full of secrets. Today, we understand much about what we see and gaze in awe. Yet, there is still much undiscovered phenomena and much to learn. We might never fully comprehend all that goes on in the heavens.

The stars and other objects in the sky have given rise to many superstitions, legends, and untrue "facts," many originated in early times yet continue in some form today. Should surgery not be scheduled during a full Moon because blood flows quicker? Does the movement of heavenly bodies determine your fate? Are there more violent crimes committed during a full Moon? Werewolves and the full Moon, vampires and sunlight, man-made canals on Mars, and other fables have stirred mankind's imagination for centuries.

We do know that there are certain forces at work that cause the Earth to be affected by other astronomical bodies. We get our energy from the Sun. The Moon affects the tides. Astronomers can account for these actions through scientific investigation. But what about such pseudo-sciences as astrology?

If astronomy were a true science, then the principles used to determine the validity of any scientific law would hold up. But they do not. Science is the study of something with knowledge gained about it. It is an ongoing process of learning and information-gathering. Scientific laws can be proven by repeating experiments and always getting the same result. They are universal laws, not trickery.

In fact, the law of gravity would have to be rewritten if it was discovered that somewhere on the Earth or in the universe dropping a rock while standing would not cause the rock to fall (assuming there were no other forces acting on the rock). Astrology fails to meet these basic scientific requirements.

Astrology is the belief that the movements and positions of heavenly bodies control people's affairs, their characteristics, and their future and foretells major events such as earthquakes and wars. Many people read their horoscope in the daily newspaper, some for fun, some to plan events in their day. The Bible says to avoid astrology. Scientists warn that there is no validity to it, and they agree that it is not a true science.

PROJECT 7-1
What's Your Sign?

Overview

Many people are lured into reading their daily horoscope in the newspaper. Some hold the belief that the "words of wisdom" listed under their zodiac sign are a guide to what they should do that day. These predictions are based on the movement and position of the stars and planets. Often, horoscope predictions are very broad and unspecific. Hypothesize that horoscope predictions are so general that they apply to most people most of the time. This will be proven by tracking 12 volunteers for two weeks and comparing their reaction to random horoscope predictions you give them to what a horoscope actually predicts for them.

Materials

- 12 volunteers (friends, parents, fellow students, teachers)
- 12 small note pads (pocket pads with spiral binding is best)
- horoscope book listing daily predictions for the next 2 weeks for all 12 zodiac signs (a daily newspaper with a horoscope listing can be used)
- small tablet and pen
- large tablet

Procedure

Obtain a list of horoscope predictions for the next two weeks (you can do it every morning by reading the morning paper). Each day there will be 12 predictions, one for each of the signs in the zodiac. On a tablet, write one prediction per sheet. Place a different letter at the top of each sheet; A, B, C, to L. Use a large tablet to record the date, the letter designation you assigned, and the sign of the zodiac that it is for. For example, on the first day Capricorn's message is "No one can agree on anything," and is on the paper you assigned the letter A to.

Give 12 volunteers small spiral bound notebooks. Record the name and zodiac sign (determined by their birthday) for each of the volunteers. Next to their names, draw 14 columns, one for each day in the two-week study. On the first day, hand each of the 12 volunteers one of the day's predictions. Mix the predictions up so there is little chance that the volunteer will get the real prediction for him. In your logbook, record the letter of the day's prediction that you gave out to each volunteer. Day 1 Johnny was handed A, Billy B, Sally C, and so on.

Every day for two weeks, hand out slips of paper with the predictions on them, each in random order so that the volunteers will get a prediction for a different sign most every day. Record which volunteer gets which prediction daily. Do not let the volunteers read their horoscopes in the paper. Do not tell them anything about their predictions. Ask them to read the prediction at the beginning of the day and then in the evening record in their notebooks a "YES" if they felt the prediction was true for that day or a "NO" if they felt it was false.

At the end of the two weeks, collect the notebooks from the volunteers. Compare their answers to the predictions they had been handed. Because most of the volunteers did not receive the correct predictions, it would be expected that their notebook logs would have a lot of "NO" responses written in them. A lot of "YES" answers on days when they did not receive the prediction that was truly given for their sign would indicate that your hypothesis was correct.

Going Further

1. Have volunteers respond with a scale of 1 to 5 instead of just yes/no. Instruct volunteers to enter a 1 for completely true, a 2 for somewhat true, 3 for can't decide, 4 for somewhat false, and 5 for completely false.

2. Hypothesize that horoscope predictions are only as accurate as random can be.

PROJECT 7-2
Heavenly Effects

Overview

The full Moon has been fabled to cause effects in animals, people, and even monsters. Do people become loony when the Moon changes phases? Some people have suggested that crime is higher during the days surrounding a full Moon.

Hypothesize that people do not exhibit worse behavior during a full Moon than at other phases of the Moon.

Materials

- permission from teachers and staff members to ask them about student behavior
- logbook
- daily newspaper

Procedure

Determine the phases of the Moon over the next month using a newspaper or other source. For the next month, at the end of each school day ask as many teachers as you can get to participate in your project how they felt student behavior was for the day. Also, ask office and other staff members. Were there more disagreements than usual on the playground? Were there more problems than usual with discipline in the classrooms? Record the date, the phase of the Moon, and each volunteer's response. At the end of the month, compare the amount of student disruptions on the days surrounding the full Moon to the days surrounding other phases—first quarter, last quarter, new Moon.

Going Further

Is absenteeism greater on the days surrounding a full Moon than at other times during the month?

PROJECT 7-3

The Old Farmer's Almanac

Overview

In many areas of the world, agriculture is highly dependent on the relationship of the Sun and the Earth. The Earth's surface faces the Sun at different angles at different times of the year, which causes the change in the seasons. The Sun/Earth relationship, the calendar date, and the planting and growing requirements of food plants is most important to farmers. Since 1792, *The Old Farmer's Almanac*, the oldest continuously published periodical in North America, has published astronomical and agricultural data. Among its pages of home medical remedies, recipes, and humorous quips are exhaustive tables and charts about many aspects of nature: eclipses, earthquakes, holidays, Moon phases, vegetable planting, plant hardiness zones, weather, tides, and sunrise/sunset times.

Hypothesize that *The Old Farmer's Almanac* is an astronomical tool.

Materials

- copy of the current year's *The Old Farmer's Almanac*, available at most book stores
- paper and pencil
- optional: copies of *The Old Farmer's Almanac* from past years

Procedure

Study all areas of the book that deal with the planting of vegetables, crops, and flowers. Be on the alert for references of planting to specific calendar dates, because the calendar is an astronomical tool based on the Earth's orbit around the Sun. Statements such as "Plant your rhubarb the second week following the spring equinox" or "plant bulbs on March 3rd" are based upon astronomy and agriculture. Record such references to support your hypothesis.

You might find the 1991 edition especially supportive of your hypothesis, where on page 180, it gives planting advice based on the Moon. It suggests:

"The best time to plant flowers and vegetables that bear crops above the ground is during the LIGHT of the Moon; that is, between the day the Moon is new to the day it is full. Flowering bulbs and vegetables that bear crops below ground should be planted during the DARK of the Moon; that is, from the day after it is full to the day before it is new again."

Evaluate your references and reach a conclusion about your hypothesis.

PROJECT 7-4
We Know What Day It Is

Overview

Early societies knew much about the night sky long before the invention of satellites, photography, spectrometers, computers, radio astronomy, and other tools available to the astronomer today. A deeper understanding of the heavens requires knowledge of both astronomy and mathematics. Hypothesize that many early civilizations had gained basic scientific knowledge of astronomy long before the invention of even the telescope.

Materials

- research materials
- paper and pencil

Procedure

Construct a chart where each row is labeled with the name of an early society, such as the Chinese, Egyptians, Greeks, Mayans, and Babylonians. The columns will be labeled by letters: *A, B, C,* and so on, where each letter represents a fact of knowledge about a particular aspect of astronomy. Below the chart, list each fact and its corresponding letter. Some suggestions for knowledge facts follow:

A   They had a calendar and knew the length of a year.
B   They understood that the Earth orbited around the Sun.
C   They could predict solar eclipses.
D   They could predict lunar eclipses.
E   They knew the length of the Moon's cycle and its phases.
F   They knew of the existence of some planets.
G   They could predict the days when seasonal flooding would occur.

Figure 7-1 shows a sample chart. Your chart should include more societies and test many more facts. Are there any facts that all of them knew about or that none of them knew about? Research the answer to the statements your chart proposes. Each cell or box on the chart can then be filled with a YES or NO (or TRUE/FALSE), indicating whether or not that society understood each fact. If your

	A	B	C	D	E	F	G
Chinese							
Egyptians							
Greeks							
Mayans							
Babylonians							

Fig. 7-1. *Research important astronomical concepts that were known by early societies.*

hypothesis is correct, then the majority of cells will contain a YES response.

Going Further

1. Make similar charts and categorize them by periods in history. For example, make 10 copies of the chart but the responses will be different. One chart might indicate knowledge known before A.D. 1000. The second chart would cover from A.D. 1000 to 1099. Chart three from A.D. 1100 to 1199. Chart four from A.D. 1200 to 1299. And the sequence would continue until modern time.

2. Was there any astronomy before the written word? Investigate cave drawings worldwide. Did early man draw any astronomical objects?

PROJECT 7-5
Science Fiction

Overview

People offer theories to explain facts or physical laws they observe. This is especially true in the field of astronomy, where astronomers now admit they don't know as much as they thought they knew. There is more acknowledgment of ignorance. We thought we knew all there was to know about Neptune, for example, until at the end of the 1980s, the Voyage spacecraft flew past it and made many new discoveries (like more Moons) and proved some theories about the planet to be in error.

Learned men once theorized that the Sun orbited around the Earth. Everyone knew that was true. It was a fact that the Sun moved across the sky each day. The "Earth as the center of the universe" theory seemed to fit the observed data. But it is dangerous to assume that a theory is, in fact, a true scientific law or a true fact. If a theory is advanced and not challenged for a long time, people might mistakenly think it is fact.

Theories are sometimes made on the edge of technology and are not in the mainstream of scientific belief. Has the Earth been visited by beings from outer space? How do you explain the many UFO (unidentified flying object) sightings that were especially prevalent in the 1950s?

Hypothesize that the higher a person's educational level, the less acceptance that person will have of popular, unproven "fad" theories. This project is not intended to be pretentious or to say that one person is smarter than another. It is simply a study in behavior regarding fad theories in astronomy.

Materials

- as many adults as you can get who will answer your short questionnaire
- paper, pencil
- optional: access to a copy machine or word processing application on a personal computer

Procedure

Prepare a questionnaire that asks a person the level of his education (elementary, high school, college) along with several questions about unproven "scientific" theories. The theories should be

PROJECT 7-6
Holiday Heavens

Overview

Throughout history, observations of the sky have been linked to activities on Earth. We tend to attribute emotions, holidays, and special occasions with heavenly observations. In this project, you'll make up a list of holidays and a second list of sky conditions. These will be copied and handed out to a large sample of people. Hypothesize that most people (most being more than 50 percent) will make the same matches of holidays to sky conditions for most of the questions (more than 50 percent). Establish a percent as to what you consider "most people" to be, for example, 75 percent of the people.

Materials

- paper and pencil
- access to a copy machine

Procedure

Make up a list of holidays and special occasions in people's lives. Make up a second list of sky conditions that you think most people would attribute to the holidays. For example:

Thanksgiving	harvest moon
Christmas	clear night sky with one bright star
Halloween	full moon
4th of July	meteor showers.

How about a romantic night in June? What might a ring around the Moon be attributed to?

Once you have made up your list, organize the holidays in one column and sky conditions in a second column, but mix up the order so that the condition is not directly opposite the holiday. You might want to use a typewriter or a word processing program on a computer to make up your questionnaire. Use a copy machine to make several dozen copies to hand out.

Tabulate the percentage of people who chose the same responses and reach a conclusion about your hypothesis.

popular but unproven facts. Your questionnaire could require an "agree" or "disagree" response. A few sample questions include:

1. Beings from other worlds have visited Earth, which accounts for the thousands of UFO sightings over the years.

2. An astronomical phenomenon that we do not yet fully understand accounts for the mysterious high loss of planes, boats, and submarines in the geographic area known as the Bermuda Triangle.

3. It is likely that a comet or meteor crashed into the Earth long ago causing dust clouds that kept sunlight from warming the Earth and contributed to the extinction of dinosaurs.

Many accepted theories have no basis in fact but are believed to be true by many people. If your school science fair has a lot of participants in the astronomy field, you may want to switch your project to the "behavior" category. In that case, add additional non-astronomical statements, such as the belief in the existence of Big Foot and The Loch Ness Monster.

Test as many adults as you can. The larger the "sample size" the more integrity in the results. Reach a conclusion about your hypothesis.

Going Further

Hypothesize which holiday/sky matches will have the correct responses. Can you select matching pairs that are so obvious that most people will get a perfect paper?

PROJECT 7-7
Heavenly Hobgoblins

Overview

The science of astronomy has worked its way into just about all areas of life, especially in literature, music, and religion. Many religions of the world, both past and present, have deities in the sky. Beliefs and superstitions are often based on astronomy. Hypothesize that you can create your own superstitions based on the sky and start them as rumors among your classmates.

Materials

- paper and pencil
- a vivid imagination

Procedure

Given your knowledge of astronomy, create a list of your own superstitions and pass them around to fellow students and friends. If you base them partly on fact, they are more likely to fool people into thinking the superstitions are credible. The following are some ideas for your "homemade superstitions":

- Dreams before midnight are always nightmares.
- Don't make any baked goods that use milk on a first quarter Moon during high tide.
- Beware the day you can see the Sun and the Moon in the same sky.
- If your dog howls at a full Moon, pour salt on his feet.

Going Further

Hypothesize that one of the rumors you started will come back to you as though it were a new idea to you.

Appendix
Resources List

This resource list is compiled to give you a mail-order source for science supplies.

Carolina Biological Supply Company
> 2700 York Road
> Burlington, NC 27215
> 800-547-1733

Edmund Scientific Company
> 101 E. Gloucester Pike
> Barrington, NJ 08007
> 609-573-6250

> Free catalog available.

Fisher Scientific
> 4901 W. LeMoyne St.
> Chicago, IL 60651
> 1-800-621-4769

Frey Scientific Company
> 905 Hickory Lane
> Mansfield, OH 44905
> 1-800-225-FREY

Science Kit & Boreal Laboratories

777 East Park Drive
Tonawanda, NY 14150-6782
800-828-7777

Sargent-Welch Scientific Company

7300 North Linder Ave.
PO Box 1026
Skokie, IL 60077
312-677-0600

Heath Company

Benton Harbor, MI 49022

Sells electronic equipment, weather instruments, computers, and test equipment.

Glossary

astronomical unit—A unit of measure of distance, abbreviated AU. One AU equals 93 million miles, the average distance between the Earth and the Sun.

barycenter—The center balancing point between two bodies that are orbiting around each other, similar to the fulcrum point on a see-saw.

constellation—A group of stars man has clustered together by drawing imaginary lines connecting them. These lines form the shapes of animals, people, and mythological characters. They give us reference points in the sky.

control group—When doing experiments, a control group is the group that has all the variables maintained. For example, if you want to test the effects of carbon monoxide on plants, you must have two equally healthy plants. Both plants will receive exactly the same care and conditions (soil, sunlight, water), and one plant, the experimental plant, will receive additional carbon monoxide. The other plant is the control plant. The control plant is maintained while the experimental plant receives the variation.

equinox—In the Sun's trek from the shortest day to the longest day of sunlight and back again, there is a day when the number of hours and minutes the Sun is above the horizon equals the number below the horizon, providing an equal amount of sunlight and darkness. When this occurs in the spring, it is called the vernal equinox. When it occurs in the fall, it is called the autumnal equinox.

experiment—A planned way to test a hypothesis.

gnomon—The vertically standing object in the center of a sundial that causes a shadow to fall on the clock face and "point" to a time marking.

greenhouse effect—Sunlight warms objects and the ground but the particles in the atmosphere keep the heat from escaping, causing a warming of the Earth. Some scientists believe this may be a serious environmental concern.

Gregorian Calendar—The calendar format we use today. Established by Pope Gregory XIII, it takes into account a leap year system to keep the calendar in sync with the Earth's orbit around the Sun.

hypothesis—A theory or educated guess. "I think when asked how much they would weigh on Mars, more boys will have accurate guesses than girls."

magnitude—A scale astronomers use to measure the apparent brightness of stars and heavenly objects.

meteor—A rocklike chunk of metal and stone that travels through space.

meteorite—A rocklike chunk of metal and stone that has traveled from outer space through the Earth's atmosphere and impacted with the Earth's surface.

meteor shower—Groups of meteors that orbit the Sun and whose path the Earth passes through, giving us annual "fireworks" displays in the sky.

observation—Looking carefully.

occulation—When one apparently larger astronomical body passes between the Earth and another apparently smaller astronomical body, the larger body is said to "occult" or block the view of the smaller body. Scientists use occulations for many things, including measuring a star's size with the help of special electronic equipment.

penumbra—One of the two parts of the shadow cast into space by the Earth. The totally dark part of the shadow is called the umbra while the penumbra is the lighter area.

Polaris—The North Star, also called Polaris, appears to be an almost stationary star in the sky as observed from Earth. It is close to the North Pole and, therefore, is used as a navigation aid.

quantify—To measure.

sample size—The number of items under test. The larger the sample size, the more significant the results. Using only two plants to test a hypothesis that sugar added to water results in better growth would not yield a lot of confidence in the results. One plant might grow better simply because some plants just grow better than others.

scientific method—A step-by-step logical process for investigation. A problem is stated, a hypothesis is formed, an experiment is set up, data is gathered, and a conclusion is reached about the hypothesis based on the data gathered.

solstice—The summer solstice, falling on either June 21 or 22, marks the day when the Sun is above the horizon for the longest amount of time in the Northern Hemisphere. The winter solstice, falling on either December 21 or 22, marks the day when the Sun is above the horizon for the shortest amount of time.

specific gravity—The relationship between the weight of an object and the weight of the water it displaces. Scientists use specific gravity to compare the densities of rocks.

sun spots—Spots on the Sun that appear darker than the Sun's normal surface. These huge spots are cooler areas.

umbra—The shadow of the Earth that extends out into space. The Earth's shadow consists of two parts, the umbra, which is the totally dark area, and the penumbra.

Index

craters
    Mars, 98-99
    meteor craters, 89-90, 96-97

D

day length, 35-36
    migration of birds, 41
hemispheres, day length, solstices,
    equinoxes, 35-36
demonstrations as science projects, 3-4
density of planets, 12-13
deviation, magnetic deviation, 67-68
diffusion of light, 78
distortion
    heat and distortion, 10
    telescope size, 26-27

E

Earth
    eclipses, 45-47
    flat Earth vs. round Earth, 61
    Moon's orbit, 43-44
    Sun's position at sunrise vs. latitude
        and longitude, 48-50
    tides, 43-44
eclipses, 45-47
    penumbra and umbra, 45-47
equinoxes, 35-36, 121
ethical practices, x, 4-5
experiments (see also science projects),
    1, 122

F

field of vision, 24-25
focal length, 27

G

galaxies, Milky Way, 81
gnomons, 30, 122
gravity
    barycenter of orbiting bodies, 16-18
    comparative gravity of planets, 13
greenhouse effect, 64-66, 122
Gregorian calendar, 33-34, 122
Gregory XIII, Pope of Rome, 33-34

H

heat and distortions, 10
height calculations, surface mapping,
    100-101
hemispheres, day length, solstices,
    equinoxes, 35-36
Hipparchus, magnitude of stars, 28
holidays vs. sky conditions, 116-117
horizon
    flat Earth vs. round Earth, 61
    size of objects, illusions, 22-23
horoscopes (see astrology), 107
hourglass construction, 37-39
hypothesis, 1-2, 114-115, 122

J

judging Science Fair projects, 5-6
Julian calendar, 33-34
Julius Caesar, 33-34

L

latitude, Sun's position at sunrise,
    48-50
leap years, 33-34
light, speed of light, 12
longitude, Sun's position at sunrise,
    48-50

M

magnetic deviation, compasses, 67-68
magnification, 24-27
magnitude, 28, 122
    measurement of magnitude, 8-9
    planets, 28
    stars, 28
Mars, surface of Mars and craters, 98-99
measurements of distance in space, 12
measurements, science projects, 3
meteor, 122
meteor craters, 89-90, 96-97
    Mars, 98-99
meteor showers, 82-83, 84-85, 122
    Persieds Shower, 102-104
meteorites, 82-83, 122
    angle of entry to Earth's atmosphere,
        93-95

Other Bestsellers of Related Interest

HOMEMADE LIGHTNING:
Creative Experiments in Electronics
—R.A. Ford

Packed with fascinating facts, this book combines scientific history, electronics theory, and practical experiments to introduce you to the evolving science of electrostatics. The abundant illustrations and varied collection of creative, hands-on projects reveal the wide-ranging impact of electrostatics on motor design, plant growth, medicine, aerodynamics, photography, meteorology, and gravity research. 208 pages, 111 illustrations. Book No. 3576, $14.95 paperback, $23.95 hardcover

HOMEMADE HOLOGRAMS: The Complete Guide to Inexpensive, Do-It-Yourself Holography—John Iovine

Make your own holograms easily and inexpensively with this breakthrough book. John Iovine tells you how to produce laser-generated images plus equipment like a portable isolation table and a helium-neon laser. You'll also construct devices that can make your experiments easier and more professional, such as magnetic film holders, spatial filters, an electronic shutter, an audible electronic timer, and a laser power meter and photometer. 240 pages, 185 illustrations. Book No. 3460, $14.95 paperback, $22.95 hardcover

OPTICAL ILLUSIONS: Puzzles, Paradoxes, and Brain Teasers #4—Stan Gibilisco

Can you believe your eyes? No matter how trustworthy your eyes may be, they'll be teased, deceived, and dazzled with this newest addition to Gibilisco's popular series. This entertaining look at visual illusion features an intriguing collection of illustrations that deceive the human eye into seeing sizes, shapes, and motion that aren't there—or not seeing what is there! 130 pages, 107 illustrations. Book No. 3464, $8.95 paperback, $15.95 hardcover

THE BEGINNER'S GUIDE TO FLYING ELECTRIC-POWERED AIRPLANES
—Douglas R. Pratt

Join the fastest-growing segment of the radio-control sport flying hobby—electric-powered airplanes! More and more flyers are discovering the advantages of clean, quiet electric power, and this book can help you make that discovery too. Pratt provides all the information you need on selecting, building, and flying these high-performance machines. He tells you what's needed in the way of motors, radios, control systems, chargers, and batteries, and how to get the most out of your model. 128 pages, 93 illustrations. Book No. 3451, $12.95 paperback only

"I MADE IT MYSELF": 40 Kids' Crafts Projects—Alan and Gill Bridgewater

This easy project book will give children hours of fun crafting toys and gifts with inexpensive household materials. Children will enjoy making musical instruments, kites, dolls, cards, masks, papier-mache and painted ornaments, as well as working toys such as a wind racer, land yacht, or moon buggy. Along with easy-to-follow instructions, each project includes scale drawings, step-by-step illustrations, and a picture of the finished item. 224 pages, 165 illustrations. Book No. 3339, $11.95 paperback, $19.95 hardcover

GORDON McCOMB'S GADGETEER'S GOLDMINE!: 55 Space-Age Projects
—Gordon McComb

This exciting collection of electronic projects features experiments ranging from magnetic levitation and lasers to high-tech surveillance and digital communications. You'll find instructions for building such useful items as a fiberoptic communications link, a Geiger counter, a laser alarm system, and more. All designs have been thoroughly tested. Suggested alternative approaches, parts lists, sources, and components are also provided. 432 pages, 274 illustrations. Book No. 3360, $18.95 paperback, $29.95 hardcover

PHYSICS FOR KIDS: 49 Easy Experiments with Optics
—Robert W. Wood

Young readers ages 8–13 will enjoy these quick and easy experiments that provide a thorough introduction to what light is, how it behaves, and how it can be put to work. Wood provides projects including: making a kaleidoscope and a periscope, an ice lens, and a pinhole camera; and learning why stars twinkle, and how a mirror works. Projects produce results often in less than 30 minutes and require only common household items to complete. 178 pages, 164 illustrations. Book No. 3402, $9.95 paperback, $16.95 hardcover

PHYSICS FOR KIDS: 9 Easy Experiments with Heat
—Robert W. Wood

This volume introduces thermodynamics, or the physics of heat, to students ages 8–13. By performing these safe, simple experiments, kids can then begin to understand the principles of conduction, convection, and radiation. Experiments show students how to: make a thermometer, make invisible ink, measure body heat, pull a wire through an ice cube, all quick, safe, and inexpensive, with results in less than 30 minutes. 160 pages, 162 illustrations. Book No. 3292, $9.95 paperback, $16.95 hardcover

Prices Subject to Change Without Notice.

Look for These and Other TAB Books at Your Local Bookstore

To Order Call Toll Free 1-800-822-8158
(in PA, AK, and Canada call 717-794-2191)

or write to TAB Books, Blue Ridge Summit, PA 17294-0840.

Title	Product No.	Quantity	Price

☐ Check or money order made payable to TAB Books

Charge my ☐ VISA ☐ MasterCard ☐ American Express

Acct. No. _____ Exp. _____

Signature: _____

Name: _____

Address: _____

City: _____

State: _____ Zip: _____

Subtotal $ _____

Postage and Handling
($3.00 in U.S., $5.00 outside U.S.) $ _____

Add applicable state and local
sales tax $ _____

TOTAL $ _____

TAB Books catalog free with purchase; otherwise send $1.00 in check or money order and receive $1.00 credit on your next purchase.

Orders outside U.S. must pay with international money order in U.S. dollars.

TAB Guarantee: If for any reason you are not satisfied with the book(s) you order, simply return it (them) within 15 days and receive a full refund.   **BC**